IELTS

Preparation and Practice

Reading and Writing
GENERAL TRAINING MODULE

Vladimir Pejovic
Michael Nicklin
Peggy Read

INDONESIA AUSTRALIA LANGUAGE FOUNDATION

OXFORD
UNIVERSITY PRESS

OXFORD

UNIVERSITY PRESS

253 Normanby Road, South Melbourne, Victoria 3205, Australia

Oxford University Press is a department of the University of Oxford.
It furthers the University's objective of excellence in research, scholarship,
and education by publishing worldwide in
Oxford New York

Auckland   Cape Town   Dar es Salaam   Hong Kong   Karachi
Kuala Lumpur   Madrid   Melbourne   Mexico City   Nairobi
New Delhi   Shanghai   Taipei   Toronto

With offices in

Argentina   Austria   Brazil   Chile   Czech Republic   France   Greece
Guatemala   Hungary   Italy   Japan   Poland   Portugal   Singapore
South Korea   Switzerland   Thailand   Turkey   Ukraine   Vietnam

OXFORD is a trade mark of Oxford University Press
in the UK and in certain other countries

National Library of Australia
Cataloguing-in-Publication data:

Pejovic, Vladimir.
IELTS preparation and practice: reading and writing.

ISBN 0 19 554094 8.
ISBN 978 0 19 554094 9.

1. English language – Textbooks for foreign speakers.
2. International English Language Testing System. 3. English language –
Examinations, questions, etc. I. Nicklin, Michael. II. Read, Peggy. III.
Title. IV. Title: International English Language Testing System
preparation and practice. (Series: IELTS preparation and practice).

428

Typeset by Stephen Chan
Printed through Bookpac Production Services, Singapore

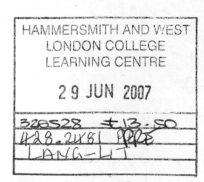

Contents

Preface

How to Use this Book

There are five main sections in this book. Each section looks at a different section of the IELTS General Training Module Reading and Writing tests.

At the beginning of each chapter there is a *Demonstration* to show you how a skilled reader and writer of English would answer the questions quickly and confidently. Instead of trying to answer the Demonstration questions by yourself, you should follow carefully the steps set out in the *How to Answer* section. In this way you will develop an understanding of the most efficient test strategies.

The *Analysis and Practice* section comes after the Demonstration and it is here the skills and strategies from the Demonstration will be explained in detail. You will have an opportunity to practise what you have learned in various activities; and, since working effectively in a limited time is very important in tests, each activity has a *Time target*. The Time target gives you a suggested time limit for completing the activity. Follow the instructions for each activity and when you have finished, check your answers in the *Answer Key* at the back of the book.

There are also *Practice Reading and Writing tests* for you to attempt once you have completed all the activities. There is a sample Reading *answer sheet* on page 155 for you to photocopy and use each time that you do a Practice Reading test. The answers for these tests are also included in the Answer Key.

General Training Reading

About the Reading Test

The IELTS General Training Reading test takes 60 minutes. It is divided into three sections.

- **Section 1** has short texts which come from advertisements, timetables, instruction manuals and the like.
- **Section 2** has longer texts (usually two texts of about 500 words each) which give information and advice about education and training.
- **Section 3** has one longer text (about 700 words) with more complex language and structure. The text will be about a general topic and will come from sources like general interest magazines.

There are between 38 and 42 questions to answer. The questions may come *before* or *after* the reading texts. There is a variety of questions. Often there are examples of how to answer the questions.

You may mark or write on the question paper, but all answers must be written on the answer sheet.

Section 1

For Section 1, you should use the following three-step strategy:

Step 1   Look at the text quickly
         (Survey the text)

Step 2   Read the instructions and the question(s)

Step 3   Find the answer

We will now look at a demonstration of how to apply this strategy to various Section 1 questions. Later, the strategies will be discussed in more detail and you will be able to practise them.

Demonstration—Text and Questions

Do not read the following text and questions first. Go directly to the *How to Answer* section which will show you the most efficient way of answering the questions.

YOUR POST OFFICE
at your service

At our main offices we are introducing, where appropriate, a number of changes to help improve the standard of service provided to our customers.

Similar developments are taking place at many of our agency offices.

Improvements:

- more staff at peak periods for faster service
- a single queuing system for fairer service
- special service windows for some transactions
- Post-Shops in main offices with their own separate service till for greeting cards, stationery, stamps and gifts
- the refurbishment of a number of main offices to provide a better environment
- new vending machine services such as cash-change machines, and phonecard and stamp dispensers for faster service
- extended opening hours at selected main offices
- a new range of air package services.

Questions 1–3

Do the following statements agree with the information given in the reading passage above? Write:

TRUE	*if the statement is true*
FALSE	*if the statement is false*
NOT GIVEN	*if the information is not given in the passage*

in the correct boxes on your answer sheet.

1 All offices will have more staff throughout the day.

2 There will be special service windows for cash transactions at all main offices.

3 It will be possible to obtain some items from machines in many offices.

Question 4

*Using **NO MORE THAN THREE WORDS** answer the following question.*

4 Which change will ensure that the customers are treated more fairly?

Question 5

*Choose the correct answer by writing **A, B, C, or D**.*

5 Which offices will stay open longer?

A	all offices	**B**	all main offices
C	some main offices	**D**	some agency offices

How to Answer

BEFORE YOU ANSWER ANY QUESTIONS

Step 1—Look at the text quickly (survey the text)
The heading tells you that the text is about *service* at post offices. The subheading and the points listed below it show *eight improvements* to the services.

QUESTION 1

Step 2—Read the instructions and the question
The instructions for questions 1–3 tell you to write *True*, *False* or *Not Given* on the answer sheet.

You are looking for specific information in the passage. The key words for question one are:

<u>All offices</u> will have <u>more staff throughout</u> the day.

The question is about *more* (additional) *staff*. You should also note that the question specifies *all* (not just some) *offices* and it also mentions *throughout* the day (that is, *all* day, not just part of the day).

Step 3—Find the answer
The best way to find the answer is to look quickly through the text for the key words or their **synonyms** (words with similar meaning). Then, read the phrase or sentence that contains those words.

Looking for the word 'office', in the first section of the text you find that the changes are being introduced in 'our main offices' and '**many** of our agency offices'. It seems that the changes do **not** refer to **all** offices.

The word 'staff' is in the first improvement listed. It says there are 'more staff at peak periods'. This means that there are only more staff at the busiest times of the day and **not** all day. Therefore, the answer is FALSE.

QUESTION 2

Step 2—Read the question
The key words are underlined:

There will be <u>special service windows</u> for <u>cash transactions</u> at <u>all main</u> offices.

You need to find information about *special service windows*, namely: their functions (are they used for cash transactions?) and where they are located (are they at *all main* offices?).

Step 3—Find the answer
'Special service windows' are mentioned in the third point, but *cash* transactions are not mentioned. There is no information in the text about what kinds of transactions take place. Nor is there any information about whether these windows will be at *all main* post offices. Therefore, the correct answer is NOT GIVEN.

QUESTION 3

Step 2—Read the question
The key words are:

It will be possible to <u>obtain some items from machines.</u>

You should search the text for the word 'machines' or synonyms.

Step 3—Find the answer
Point 6 mentions 'cash machines' and 'phonecard and stamp dispensers'. So you can *obtain* (get) cash (one item) from a machine, but what are 'dispensers'? The text tells you that they provide a faster service, and vending machines do that, so it is reasonable to guess that a dispenser is a kind of machine. So, you **can** get *some items* from machines. Therefore, the correct answer is TRUE.

Note: If you don't know the meaning of a word, you may be able to work out its meaning by looking at the words around it. This technique is called *guessing from context.* It is a very important skill and will be discussed in detail at the end of Section 2.

QUESTION 4

Step 2—Read the instructions and the question
Here you are instructed to write your answer in **up to three words** (i.e. one, two or three words).

The key words in the question 4 are:

<u>Which change</u> will ensure that the <u>customers</u> are <u>treated more fairly</u>?

All of the changes mentioned in the text are to 'help improve the standard of service'. Which one provides *fairer* service?

Step 3—Find the answer
Point one provides 'faster service'. Point two provides 'fairer service'. You don't need to read further than this. The answer is 'single queuing system' (3 words).

QUESTION 5

Step 2—Read the instructions and the question
The instruction tells you to write a **letter** (A, B, C or D), not a **word**.
The key words in the question are underlined:

Which offices will stay open longer?

The answer choices also help here. Factors such as the type of office (*main* or *agency*) and whether it is *some* or *all* offices are relevant.

Step 3—Find the answer
We have already looked for the key word 'office' (in question 1) and found that the changes are being introduced in 'our main offices' (sentence 1) and '**many** of our agency offices'. It seems that the changes do **not** refer to **all** offices.
Looking quickly for *stay open longer* or synonyms, we find 'extended opening hours' in the seventh improvement. However, it mentions only '*selected* main offices'. The answer is therefore **C**—'some main offices'.

Analysis and Practice

The three different kinds of questions used in the Demonstration are the most common question types in Section 1 of the Reading test.
* True-False-Not Given (questions 1–3)
* short answer of no more than three words (question 4)
* Multiple choice (question 5)

Following the three-step strategy:
* survey the text
* read the instructions and the question(s)
* find the answers
is usually the fastest and surest way of doing the kinds of questions you will find in Section 1. We will now look at each of these steps in more detail.

STEP 1—SURVEY THE TEXT

You can quickly obtain a lot of useful information about a text by just looking at:
* the title
* section headings or subheadings
* any words in special print (**bold**, *italics*, CAPITALS or underlined)
* any diagrams, tables or pictures
* any unusual features of the text (e.g. layout or boxed text).

Surveying tells you about the topic or subject of the text. It may also tell you something about how the text is organised (subheadings are especially useful). Surveying may also tell you something about the writer's purpose—whether the intention is to give instructions, to compare, to give information, and so on.

ACTIVITY 1

In the following text you can see only the layout, the title, the subheadings, the illustration and a few words in special print above the illustration. These are the features of the text you look at when you survey. With only this information, answer the questions that follow the text.

Time target: up to 2 minutes

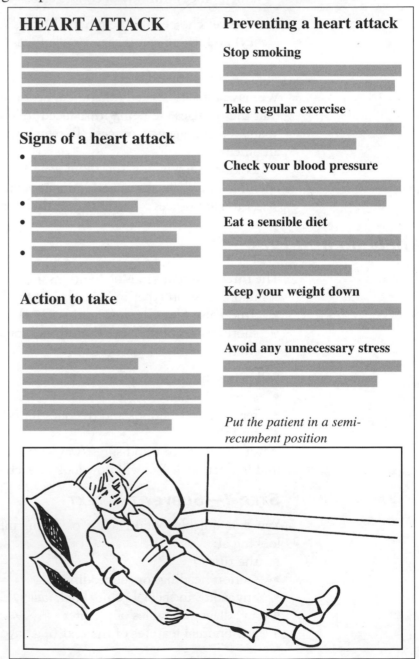

HEART ATTACK

Signs of a heart attack

Action to take

Preventing a heart attack

Stop smoking

Take regular exercise

Check your blood pressure

Eat a sensible diet

Keep your weight down

Avoid any unnecessary stress

Put the patient in a semi-recumbent position

1   What is the text about?

   A   the heart

   B   smoking

   C   healthy habits

   D   heart attacks

2   How many signs of a heart attack are described?

3   Name two things that are not good for your heart.

4   The semi-recumbent position is dangerous for someone who has had a heart attack. Is this statement TRUE, FALSE or is the information NOT GIVEN?

Check your answers with the Answer Key.

The next activity gives you a complete text, but **do not read the complete text in the normal way.** You should be able to answer the questions below the text by only *surveying* the text.

ACTIVITY 2

Survey the following text and then answer the questions using the strategy described in the Demonstration.

Time target: 2 minutes

If you travel by bus, car, boat, plane or train with your children, make sure that travel-sickness doesn't spoil the journey.

Take a of packet of EASY RIDERS

Easy Riders are **chocolate flavoured** but they aren't lollies. They're children's travel-sickness tablets.

The tablets contain doses that are **safe for children**, so there's no danger of overdose if you follow the instructions on the packet.

You can give EASY RIDERS to your children as a preventative measure or wait to see if travel-sickness develops and then give one.

So if you're taking your children on a journey, don't forget the EASY RIDERS.

An easy ride for your children means an easier ride for you.

Available from your local chemist or drugstore.

Produced by

LUCKY PHARMACEUTICAL CO.

Questions 1–3

1   Easy Riders are:

    A   a kind of game

    B   a travel company

    C   a kind of medicine

    D   special bus tickets

2   Name one place where you can buy Easy Riders?

3   Who are Easy Riders for?

Check your answers with the Answer Key.

STEP 2—READ THE INSTRUCTIONS AND THE QUESTION

Reading the instructions

It is very important that you read the instructions carefully. If you do not follow the instructions and write your answer the wrong way—for example, if the instructions tell you to write a **letter** (A, B, C) and you write a **word**—your answer may be marked incorrect.

ACTIVITY 3

Here are some questions about the first part of this book. The questions are followed by a candidate's sample answers. Is the information in each answer correct? Try to check the answer by scanning earlier parts of this book. Also, check that the questions have been answered in the correct way. If not, what is wrong with them?

Questions 1–3

*Using **NO MORE THAN THREE WORDS**, answer the following questions.*

1   Who published this book? _Oxford University Press_

2   Where must the candidates write their answers in the IELTS Reading test? _On the official answer sheet_

3   Name one thing a reader can learn about a text by surveying it.

The topic, organisation and writer's purpose

Questions 4 –6

Read the statements below. Write:

TRUE   *if the statement is true*

FALSE   *if the statement is false*

NOT GIVEN   *if there is no information about this in the text*

4   The first section of the Reading test has longer texts than the other sections in the test. _False_

5   Candidates should read instructions carefully before writing their answers. _T_

6   Most IELTS Reading texts come from British publications.

no information

Questions 7 –8

*Answer the questions by choosing the appropriate letters **A–D**.*

7   If the instruction says 'USING NO MORE THAN THREE WORDS', how many words should you write? _one, two or three_

    A more than three   **B**   exactly three

    C one, two or three   **D**   less than three

8   Which of the following do you NOT do when surveying a text?

    A read the title

    B read most of the words in the text carefully

    C look at illustrations and diagrams

    D read section headings and/or subheadings

    _B_

Check your answers with the Answer Key.

In the real IELTS Test, it is also essential that you write your answer **in the correct box** on the answer sheet. You should keep checking that you are writing every answer in the box that has the same number as the question. You will have a chance to practise this when you do the Practice tests at the end of this book.

Reading the question
You should try to identify:
- the topic (the subject, or what the question is about)
- exactly what you need to know about the topic.

It is a good idea to <u>underline</u> the key words in the question as you read. (Remember that you can write on the question booklet.) Look back at the Demonstration answers for Reading Sample 1 to see how you should do this. For multiple choice questions you may have to underline key words in the answer choices as well as in the question.

STEP 3—LOOKING FOR THE ANSWERS

In exams you do not have time to read every word carefully. **Remember that your task is to answer the questions, *not* to understand *all* of the text.** It is often only necessary to **read *a small part of the text* carefully** to answer the questions.

The best way to find details quickly is to use *scanning*. Scanning is searching for key words or synonyms by looking quickly through the text. Your eyes move across and down through the text without reading in the normal way. For example, you *scan* when you look for a word in a dictionary. You do not read every word as you search for the word(s) you want.

It is easiest to scan for numbers or words which start with capital letters (such as most names) because these stand out in a text.

ACTIVITY 4

Answer the questions that follow the next text by scanning. Use the names and numbers to find the answers to the questions.

Time target: 3 minutes

 SOURCES OF VITAMINS

Most vitamins we need are available in sufficient quantities in vegetables and fruits. To give some examples, we need about 50mg of vitamin C per day, and we can get it readily from citrus <u>fruits</u>, tomatoes and <u>green</u> vegetables. Vitamin A (800mcg per day) is also available mainly from green vegetables.

Some vitamins, however, can only be found in sufficient quantities in animal products. For example, vitamin B12, of which we need about 2mcg per day for healthy red blood cells, is usually obtained from liver, sardines and eggs. The

15mg of niacin we need is most readily obtained from <u>lean</u> meats and fish.

Vitamin D is unusual in that it is usually produced by our own bodies after receiving sunlight on our <u>skin</u>. The growth and development of bones and teeth relies partly on us having <u>10mcg</u> of vitamin D per day.

1   What is one source of Vitamin A?

2   We need 15mg per day of which vitamin?

3   We need 2mcg per day of which vitamin?

4   How much Vitamin D should we have per day?

Check your answers with the Answer Key.

Scanning for normal words is a bit more difficult than scanning for numbers or names, but if you practise you will be able to do it more quickly and efficiently.

ACTIVITY 5

Go back to the text 'Easy Riders' extract on page 7. Answer the following question by scanning only.

1   How many times is the word 'children' mentioned in the text?

Time target: 20 seconds

Check your answer in the Answer Key.

ACTIVITY 6

Now try to answer some IELTS-type questions about the 'Easy Riders' text. First, survey the text (Step 1) again. Read the instructions and the question (Step 2). Decide which words from the following questions are key words and then scan for those key words or their synonyms to find the answer (Step 3).

Time target: 2 minutes

Questions 1–3

Do the following statements agree with the information given in the Reading text?

Write:

TRUE   *if the statement is true*

FALSE   *if the statement is false*

NOT GIVEN   *if the information is not given in the text*

1   Easy Riders can be used for land, sea or air travel.

2   Easy Riders are chocolates.

3   An overdose of this medicine is not dangerous.

Question 4

*Choose the correct answer by writing **A, B, C or D**.*

4   When should you give Easy Riders to children?

   A only before the journey begins

   B only when the child is sick

   C both one before the journey starts and another during the journey if there are symptoms of travel sickness

   D either one before the journey begins or one during the journey if there are symptoms of travel sickness

Check your answers with the Answer Key.

ACTIVITY 7

In this activity we will again practise scanning for synonyms. The complete 'Heart Attacks' text follows. Do not read the text in the normal way. Look at the underlined words and phrases below and scan for their synonyms in the text.

Time target: 3 minutes

1   <u>The person who has had the heart attack</u> may not be conscious.

2   <u>Check</u> the heart rate and breathing.

3   Try to <u>lose weight</u>.

4   Victims of heart attacks have <u>difficulty breathing</u>.

5   Pain may <u>begin suddenly</u> in the centre of the chest.

6   The person should sit in a way that does not put too much <u>pressure</u> on the chest.

Check your answers in the Answer Key.

HEART ATTACK

A heart attack is caused by a reduction in the blood supply to the heart muscles. This is most commonly caused by a blood clot obstructing an artery in the heart. Heart attacks can be mild or severe. If you suspect that someone has had a heart attack call for medical help immediately.

Signs of a heart attack

- Sudden onset of pain in the centre of the chest. The pain will be vice-like, crushing. It could be confused with very severe indigestion. It may spread upwards and outwards to the throat, jaw and arms.

- Shortness of breath.

- The pulse rate may become faster or weak and irregular.

- The casualty will become pale and sweaty and show signs of shock (page 39).

Action to take

Call an ambulance. Check the heartbeat and breathing. If it has stopped, then commence external chest compression and mouth-to-mouth ventilation immediately (see page 6).

If the casualty is conscious, move gently and as little as possible into a comfortable position. A semi-recumbent position (shown below) is the best. It is easiest for the casualty to breathe in this position and takes some of the strain off the heart.

Loosen any clothing around the neck and reassure that help is on its way. Monitor heart rate and breathing regularly until help arrives. If the person becomes unconscious move to the recovery position.

Preventing a heart attack

Stop smoking

Smoking is the major cause of heart disease. It damages the arteries and the circulation of blood. Stop immediately.

Take regular exercise

Steady and regular exercise is very beneficial. Walking is a good form of exercise.

Check your blood pressure

High blood pressure can cause a heart attack. Ask your doctor to check your blood pressure.

Eat a sensible diet

Cut down on the amount of fatty foods that you eat. Cut fat off meat.

Keep your weight down

If you are overweight, this puts an extra strain on the heart. Shed those excess pounds now!

Avoid unnecessary stress

Do not push yourself to unrealistic targets. Be sensible about the amount of work you do each day.

Put the patient in a semi-recumbent position

ACTIVITY 8

Now try to do some IELTS-type questions about the 'Heart Attacks' text. First, survey the text quickly again (Step 1). Read the instructions and the question (Step 2) and then finally scan for the answer (Step 3).

Time target: 5 minutes

Questions 1–2

Choose the appropriate letters A–D.

1   What causes a heart attack?

    A too much blood getting to the heart muscle

    B not enough blood getting to the heart muscle

    C an artery in the heart

    D an obstructed heart muscle

2   Which of the following is *not* a sign of a heart attack?

    A pain in the centre of the chest

    B indigestion

    C breathing difficulties

    D fast or weak and irregular pulse rate

Questions 3–4

Complete the sentences below with words taken from the reading passage. Use NO MORE THAN THREE WORDS for each answer.

3   If you think someone has had a heart attack, try to get

_____

4   After calling an ambulance, check the casualty's

_____

Questions 5–7

Do the statements below agree with the information in the Reading passage?

Write:

TRUE   *if the statement is true*

FALSE   *if the statement is false*

NOT GIVEN   *if the information is not given in the passage*

Example	Answer
External chest compression and mouth-to-mouth ventilation should only be given by someone with medical training.	**NOT GIVEN**

5   Avoid moving the casualty more than necessary.

6   Sitting in a semi-recumbent position strains the heart.

7   Loosening clothing around the neck reduces the casualty's blood pressure.

Check your answers with the Answer Key.

Summary—Section 1

QUESTION TYPES

The most common question types in Section 1 of the Reading test are:
• multiple choice
• True, False or Not Given
• short answers (of no more than 3 words).

STRATEGIES

Step 1 Survey (look quickly at) the text
> • look for any parts of the text which stand out such as titles or pictures

Step 2 Read the instructions and the questions
- make sure you know *how* you must answer
- underline the key words in the question (and instructions)

Step 3 Look for the answers
- scan for key words and synonyms by looking over the text
- do not read every word
- numbers and words beginning with capital letters are the easiest to scan for

Section 2

To complete Section 2 of the Reading test successfully you should follow a three-step strategy similar to the one practised in Section 1.

> Step One   Survey the text
>
> Step Two   Read the questions
>
> Step Three   Answer the questions by **scanning** for specific information
>
>   or
>
>   Identifying main ideas by **skimming**

In this section you will learn the skill of *skimming*. Scanning and skimming are used by native speakers to get information from texts more quickly.

A common cause of failure in the IELTS Reading test is bad time management, resulting in candidates not finishing all the questions. Unless you are a very fast reader, **you will not have time to read the texts in Sections 2 and 3 carefully from beginning to end**. It is, however, not necessary to do so. You only need to read enough to find the answers to the questions.

So, for the following demonstration, do not read the demonstration text and questions first. Go directly to the *How to Answer* section on page 20, and refer back to the reading text as instructed.

Demonstration—Text and Questions

THINGS TO EXPECT IN AUSTRALIA

A   **Australia is a relatively safe place**, something which surveys of overseas students have shown that they value greatly. As in most of the industrialised countries, Australia has experienced a serious economic recession making many people unemployed. This has caused a small increase in the amount of petty crime, but in comparison with the USA, UK, Europe or almost anywhere else in the Western world the problem remains limited.

B   **The opportunity to work while studying** in order to help cover expenses is one which overseas students welcome. Australia is comparatively generous in this regard, especially since changes to government policy in February 1991. All overseas students, irrespective of which country they come from and what they intend to study, may work for up to 20 hours per week during semesters and full-time during vacations and other course breaks. Part-time study is not permitted on a student visa.

C **Finding work in a different country can be trying**, and if it is essential for survival the pressure that it creates can be a worry. Most campuses maintain a part-time work agency, but the number of jobs available from place to place varies. Generally, it is not easy to find work at the moment because Australia is experiencing an economic recession. More than half of Australia's visiting students say that they take advantage of the right to work, but it is hard to know for certain how much they do or what they earn.

D **Multiculturalism is official government policy** despite the strong British heritage stemming from Australia's colonial origins. There are now more than 100 different ethnic groups represented in Australia, and much of the increase in diversity occurred during the last generation or two. Just after the Second World War, Australia had a population of only 7.1 million. Now there are more than 17 million people; new immigrants and their children account for about half of that growth. One authority has written recently: 'On the whole the interaction of old and new Australians has been achieved with a minimum of conflict—migration has worked.'

E **The friendliness of the Australian people** is something which surveys of tourists show to be one of the main and most favourable impressions of visitors. Overseas students back that up, as student survey results show. In 1984 more than 1000 overseas students were asked their opinion of Australians, and were also asked to describe the attitudes of Australians towards them. The results of the survey appear in Figure 1.

Figure 1

Attitudes of overseas students towards Australians

Positive	
like them a lot	20 %
tend to like them	56
Indifferent	21
Negative	
tend to dislike them	2
dislike them a lot	-

Attitudes of Australians to overseas students

Positive

very accepting	16%
fairly friendly	62

Indifferent 13

Negative

a bit unfriendly	8
very unfriendly	1

Source: Committee for Review of Overseas Student Policy, pp 292–3

Surveys have found that between 80 and 90 per cent of overseas students who have studied in Australia would recommend that friends and other family members should study there. Similar proportions say that if they were to migrate permanently they would choose Australia.

Questions 1–4

The passage has five paragraphs labelled A to E. Choose the most suitable heading for each paragraph from the list by writing the appropriate number (i–viii).

Note: *There are more headings than paragraphs so you will not use all of them. You may use any of the headings more than once.*

List of headings

i   Jobs are Hard to Find

ii   Security

iii Racial Prejudice

iv   Work Regulations for Overseas Students

v   Part-time Students

vi   Cultural Diversity

vii Positive Impressions of Overseas Students Towards Australians

viii The Australian Personality

Example	Answer
paragraph A	ii

1	paragraph B	**2**	paragraph C
3	paragraph D	**4**	paragraph E

Questions 5–8

Using information from the reading passage, complete the following sentences in **NO MORE THAN THREE WORDS**.

5   Australia's economic recession has led to an increase in

_____

6   In February 1991, the Australian Government passed a law permitting overseas students

_____

7   A holder of a student visa is not allowed to

_____

8   Seventy-eight per cent of Australians had positive feelings about

_____

How to Answer

BEFORE YOU TRY TO ANSWER ANY QUESTIONS

Step 1—Survey the text

The title, 'Things to expect in Australia', tells you that the text contains information for visitors to Australia.

The words in **bold** type at the beginning of each paragraph give you a good idea of what kind of information is given in that paragraph.

	Topic
Australia is a relatively safe place...	safety, security
The opportunity to work while studying...	students working
Finding work in a different country can be trying...	finding a job overseas
Multiculturalism is official government policy...	many cultures in Australia
The friendliness of the Australian people...	Australians

Figure 1 is part of the last paragraph. It gives information about what over-seas students think about Australians and what Australians think about overseas students.

QUESTION 1

Step 2—Read the instructions and the question
For questions 1–4, you must match the **headings** with the **paragraphs**. The purpose of the heading is to indicate the main idea or topic of the paragraph.

To answer the question you must write only a number (i,ii,iii etc.), **not** the complete heading. Look at the example:

Example	Answer
paragraph A	**ii**

Step 3—Look for the answer
1   Look at the first sentence of a paragraph. (Since paragraph A has been done in the example go directly to paragraph B.)

You already know from the survey that the topic of paragraph B is *students working*. The rest of the first sentence:

> **The opportunity to work while studying** in order to help cover expenses is one which overseas students welcome.

gives the additional information that the writer is referring to *overseas students working* (to get extra money for living expenses).
2   With this idea in mind, look quickly through the rest of the paragraph. This confirms that the topic of the paragraph is *students and work* and the main idea is Australian government policy and regulations on this topic.
3   Consider the list of headings. Heading i—Jobs are Hard to Find—is relevant to the topic *work*, but the idea of work being hard to find does not match the main idea of the paragraph. Heading iv—Work Regulations for Overseas Students—is an accurate description of the topic and main idea of paragraph B and is therefore the correct answer.

QUESTION 2

Step 2—Read the question
Step 3—Look for the answer
1   The first sentence in paragraph C is:

> **Finding work in a different country can be trying**, and if it is essential for survival the pressure that creates can be a worry.

We can guess that the main topic of this paragraph is *the pressure (or the prob-lems) of finding work.*
2   Keeping this main topic in mind, look quickly through the rest of the para-graph. This confirms that the topic is still *the difficulty of finding work.*
3   Look through the *remaining* headings (not headings ii and iv since they have already been used). Jobs are Hard to Find (**i**) is the correct answer.

QUESTION 3

Step 2—Read the question
Step 3—Look for the answer
1 The first sentence of paragraph D:

> **Multiculturalism is official government policy** despite the strong British heritage stemming from Australia's colonial origins.

tells us the paragraph probably talks about there being *many cultures* and *government policy* in relation to those cultures.
2 With this main idea in mind, look quickly through the rest of the paragraph. This confirms that the topic is still the *mixture of migrant groups*.
3 Look through the remaining headings. The headings Part-time Students (v), Positive Impressions of Overseas Students Towards Australians (vii) and The Australian Personality (viii) can be rejected immediately because they are in no way related to the topic of the paragraph.

Heading iii, Racial Prejudice, is related to the topic of the paragraph, but prejudice is a negative idea, and in the paragraph the writer uses positive words and phrases, 'interaction', 'achieved', 'migration has worked'. Heading vi, Cultural Diversity, is also related to the topic. If you do not know what 'diversity' means (it means variety) then the word 'culture' is enough to give you a match here. So the correct answer is **vi**.

QUESTION 4

Step 2—Read the question
Step 3—Look for the answer
1 The first sentence says that tourists have *favourable* (positive) *impressions* (opinions) about Australians being friendly.

> **The friendliness of the Australian people** is something which surveys of tourists show to be one of the main and most favourable impressions of visitors.

2 Look at the rest of the paragraph and the figure. The use of the results of surveys and students' opinions supports the main idea that visitors like Australia and its people.
3 Of the remaining headings: heading iii, Racial Prejudice, is negative so cannot be correct and heading viii, The Australian Personality, is possible if you look only at the first sentence of the paragraph. However, the rest of the paragraph, including Figure 1, is about the positive impressions of overseas students. Heading **vii**, Positive Impressons of Overseas Students Towards Australians, is the correct answer.

QUESTION 5

Step 2—Read the instructions and the question
The instructions tell you to complete the given sentence in *no more than three words*. Your answer should be grammatically correct. Since you are looking for specific information from the text you have to scan the text for the answer.

The key words in question 5 are underlined:

Australia's <u>economic recession</u> has led to an <u>increase</u> in …

You are looking for a consequence or result of economic recession, in particular something which has increased.

Step 3—Look for the answer
If you know approximately where to begin scanning in the relevant paragraph, you will be able to find the key words you are looking for much more efficiently and quickly. In this instance there are two ways to find the answer.

You might remember seeing the words 'economic recession' in paragraph C, and if so you can go directly to this paragraph and begin scanning for the key words or their synonyms. Even if you did not see the words in the text, you might still be able to guess that the subject of economic recession is relevant to the paragraph which talks about the problems of finding work in Australia (paragraph C).

In paragraph C, the relevant sentence says that 'it is not easy to find work at the moment' because of the economic recession. If jobs are hard to find, this means that unemployment has increased—the answer would be **unemployment**.

If you have no idea where to start scanning, you should start at the beginning of the text. If you begin scanning from the beginning of the text you see that the word 'recession' is also mentioned in paragraph A. Here it says that the recession has made 'many people unemployed'. You should write only the word 'unemployment' on your answer sheet.

QUESTION 6

Step 2—Read the question
The key words in the question are:

In <u>February 1991</u>, the Australian <u>Government</u> passed a <u>law permitting</u> overseas students …

Step 3—Find the answer
Scanning for the date (**numbers** are much easier to find in a text than key **words**), we find it in paragraph B. In the sentence with the date, and the sentence before it, we see that the government made it easier for overseas students to work. The correct answer is therefore **to work.**

QUESTION 7

Step 2—Read the question
The key words in the question are:

A holder of a <u>student visa</u> is <u>not allowed to</u> …

Step 3—Find the answer
You may remember seeing the words 'student visa' in the paragraph about working while studying (paragraph B). Even if you did not see these words in the text, you might still be able to guess that the subject of student visas is relevant to this paragraph. If this, too, is not clear, then you should start at the beginning of the text and scan for the key words above, or their synonyms.

The words 'student visa' are at the end of paragraph B. Here you will also see the words 'not permitted', which are a synonym of other key words in the question, 'not allowed'. The last sentence, 'Part-time study is not permitted on a student visa', says that you cannot study part-time on a student visa. The correct answer is therefore **study part-time**.

QUESTION 8

Step 2—Read the question
The key words are:

Seventy-eight per cent of Australians had positive feelings about …

Step 3—Find the answer
From what you already know about the text, you can guess that the answer to this question will be in the last paragraph. You should scan this paragraph for the figure 78.

Actually, the number is not mentioned in the last paragraph. The final part of the last paragraph mentions 'between 80 and 90 per cent of overseas students' but this does not help. The only other place that percentages are mentioned is in the table. The answer is in the second half of the table, which has details about the attitude of Australians toward overseas students. If you add together the percentages in the *positive* section, you get 78%. The answer is therefore **overseas students**.

Analysis and Practice

Section 2 of the Reading test usually has two reading texts. Each text usually has only one type of question. (The previous Demonstration text had two question types for convenience.) The kinds of questions most common in Section 2 are:

Questions about specific information
- completing sentences (see questions 5–8 in the Section 2 Demonstration)
- True/False/Not Given (see Section 1)
- matching pieces of specific information (there will be some examples of this in Section 3)
- other question types as in Section 1

Questions about main ideas
- matching headings with paragraphs (see questions 1–4 in the Section 2 Demonstration)
- identifying where to find information (these will be discussed later in this section)

The most efficient strategies for answering *specific information* questions are different from the strategies for *main idea* questions. Therefore, when you start Section 2 of the reading test, you should look briefly at the questions to see what type of questions they are. Then you can apply the most suitable strategies.

Also, the first part of the instructions which tell you how to answer the questions will often mention the *subject* or the *source* of the text. For an example, look at the text 'Careers Information Program' on page 36. This information can help you to understand the text more quickly.

We will now look at how to answer each of the question types mentioned opposite.

QUESTIONS ABOUT SPECIFIC INFORMATION

As in Section 1, for these questions you should:
- survey the text
- read the question
- scan for the answer.

Step 1—Survey the text
Look at:
- the title
- section headings or subheadings
- any words in special print (**bold**, *italics*, CAPITALS or <u>underlined</u>)
- any diagrams, tables or pictures in the text
- any unusual features in the text (e.g. layout or boxes).

The texts in Section 2 are usually longer than the texts in Section 1. It is therefore also useful, while surveying, to get an idea of the **organisation** of the text, namely, what topics are discussed and in what order. (Note that you are trying to identify *topics* only.) This will help you know where (in which paragraph or section) to scan later for the answer to a question.

If the text has a lot of **subheadings**, it is much easier to identify text organisation.

ACTIVITY 9

Only the title and the section headings remain of the following text. Survey the text by looking at this information and then answer the questions.

Time target: 1 minute

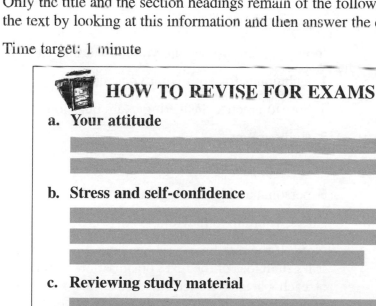

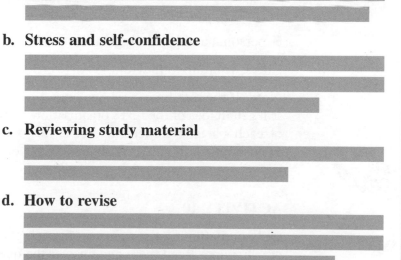

HOW TO REVISE FOR EXAMS

a. **Your attitude**

b. **Stress and self-confidence**

c. **Reviewing study material**

d. **How to revise**

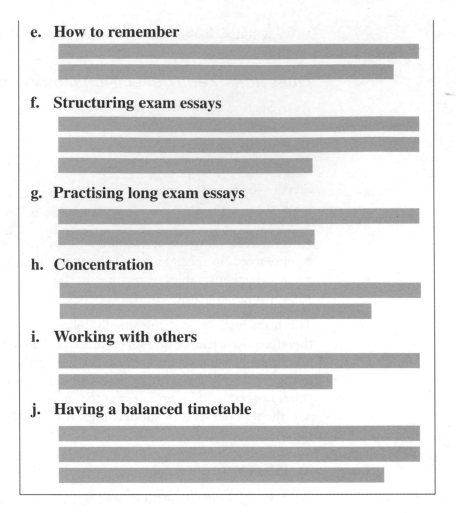

e. How to remember

f. Structuring exam essays

g. Practising long exam essays

h. Concentration

i. Working with others

j. Having a balanced timetable

Questions 1–5

In which section(s) would you look to find an answer for a question about:

1 techniques for improving your memory?

2 how to practise answering exam questions?

3 study groups?

4 study hours?

5 personal and psychological factors?

Check your answers with the Answer Key.

Note: If the text has no subheadings, or very few subheadings, then you can still get an idea of the text's organisation quickly by reading the first sentence of each paragraph. Remember the first sentence of a paragraph in many English texts will give you the main topic or main idea of that paragraph.

ACTIVITY 10

Only parts (the first sentence from each paragraph) of the following text are showing. Read them and answer the questions.

FIRST DEGREE COURSES

COURSES

1. First degrees are the first degree you can take after leaving school, unlike a higher degree or masters degree.

2. Arts, social science and pure science degrees normally last three years in England, Wales and Northern Ireland because they are designed to follow a very specialised school-leaving qualification.

3. First degree courses that include professional training take longer.

4. Apart from undergraduate courses, there is a second type of higher educational qualification in the UK known as the Higher National Diploma or HND

TEACHING AND ASSESSMENT

5. UK universities and colleges use a range of teaching methods.

    LECTURES—

    SEMINARS—

    TUTORIALS—

6. Assessment of students' work may be done in several different ways, but most universities still use some form of written examination.

7. 'Continuous assessment' is an increasingly popular method of assessment.

8. Many first degree honours courses require students to write a dissertation, which is an extended essay on a subject of the student's choice (chosen in consultation with staff).

Questions 1–5

In which paragraph would you look to answer a question about:

1 the length of certain degree courses?

2 job training?

3 the Higher National Diploma?

4 how teachers teach?

5 assessment?

Check your answers with the Answer Key.

Step 2—Read the question
Remember to:
• underline key words
• read only one question and then find the answer to that question before you read the next.

Step 3—Find the answer
For questions asking about specific information you should now *scan* for the answer.

   Because you have already surveyed the text and also now know something about how the text is organised (see Step 1), you should already have some idea where—that is, in which section or paragraph—you can find the answer.

ACTIVITY 11

Here is the complete text and questions for the 'How to Revise for Exams' extract. Answer the questions. **Do not read the whole text first**. Read a question first and then look for the answer by scanning. Focus on the paragraph or section that deals with the topic of the question.

Time target: 4–5 minutes

 HOW TO REVISE FOR EXAMS

Students learn and study in different ways. No one way best suits all students. We make the following suggestions, but they need to be interpreted flexibly.

a. Your attitude

Start with a positive frame of mind. Remind yourself why exams are necessary (to measure student performance and to assess student potential), and why you are going to do well in your exam (because you have been reasonably hard-working and have prepared intelligently).

b. Stress and self-confidence

Reduce stress and increase self-confidence. Make yourself familiar with the format of the exam. Most tests follow the pattern of earlier years. So, study past exam papers, noting exam format, the choice of questions and the time limits.

c. Reviewing study material

Review systematically. Go through all of your learning materials (class and reading notes, handouts, essays, etc.), making a careful index under major and minor headings.

d. How to revise

Revise actively, not passively. Revision means more than 're-viewing' and passing your eye across pages of notes. Active revision means using a questioning approach: do you understand what your notes mean? Follow up any points you do not understand.

e. How to remember

Learn how to recall and use your knowledge. Practise remembering ideas and making use of your knowledge. Learn to join ideas together by making connections between information from various sources.

f. Structuring exam essays

The organisation of essays is very important. One page of well-structured answer is worth ten pages of aimless text. But good exam technique only comes with practice. To do well at short exam answers you need to practise noting and organising your thoughts quickly.

g. Practising long exam essays

Get used to writing continuously for long periods without a break under exam conditions. This will help you to develop writing skills and to manage your most important resource—time.

h. Concentration

Don't daydream or drift into a negative frame of mind. Concentration depends on practice, but it also depends on keeping fit and healthy. Remember to take regular breaks for fresh air, physical exercise and refreshment. Avoid excessive tea, coffee and alcohol.

i. Working with others

Consider the value of cooperative revision. Most students

revise alone, and many become depressed because they feel they are falling behind. Others find it best to work in a revision group. Working with fellow students reminds you that you are not alone and is mutually supportive.

j. Having a balanced timetable

Maintain a balanced review timetable. Don't revise only a few topics to the exclusion of all others. Spread your revision over two or more subjects each day. Take a day off now and then as a reward. Remember, you are building yourself up to peak performance on the day of the exam.

Questions 1–5

Do the statements below agree with the information in the reading passage? In the correct boxes on your answer sheet write:

TRUE	*if the statement is true*
FALSE	*if the statement is false*
NOT GIVEN	*if there is no information about this in the text*

1 You can remember things better if you review them every day.

2 You should practise writing exam essays slowly and carefully.

3 Working in groups with other students to revise for exams is a good idea.

4 You should revise by concentrating on only one subject per day.

5 Studying old exam papers will make you more confident.

Check your answers with the Answer Key.

ACTIVITY 12

Here is the complete text and questions for the 'First Degree Courses' passage. Answer the questions. As for the previous activity, **do not read the whole text first**. Read a question first and then look for the answer by scanning. Try to focus your scanning on the paragraph or section that deals with the topic of the question.

Time target: 5 minutes

 FIRST DEGREE COURSES

COURSES

1. First degrees are the first degree you can take after leaving school, unlike a higher degree or masters degree. They are also often called undergraduate degrees.

2. Arts, social science and pure science degrees normally last three years in England, Wales and Northern Ireland because they are designed to follow a very specialised school-leaving qualification. In Scotland, they take four years because Scottish students do a less specialised school-leaving examination.

3. First degree courses that include professional training take longer. For example, medicine or veterinary science each take 5 or 6 years and architecture takes 5 to 7 years. In addition, some courses in business studies, engineering, science and technology are one year longer to allow students to undertake practical training. These are known as 'sandwich' courses and include periods of work experience in industry and commerce.

4. Apart from undergraduate courses, there is a second type of higher educational qualification in the UK known as the Higher National Diploma or HND. It lasts a year less than a degree course—either two years full time or three as a sandwich course. HNDs are vocational (or job related), so you will not find them in purely academic subjects such as history or philosophy. They are available, for example, in engineering, science subjects, business studies, hospitality and tourism management.

TEACHING AND ASSESSMENT

5. UK universities and colleges use a range of teaching methods. You might find a combination of:

    LECTURES—given to large groups of students, sometimes up to 200.

    SEMINARS—discussions between one member of staff and a small group of students on a previously arranged topic, which everyone has prepared. Often, one student reads out an essay or seminar paper, then everyone joins in the discussion.

    TUTORIALS—discussions between a member of staff and two or three students, sometimes only one.

6. Assessment of students' work may be done in several different ways, but most universities still use some form of written examination. These can last for up to three hours, in which time you have to answer three or four questions in essay form. Examinations may be held each year or may come all together at the end of the course (in which case they are known as 'finals'). Very few

institutions, however, use examinations alone, and even fewer rely solely on finals.

7. 'Continuous assessment' is an increasingly popular method of assessment. This is based on the marks a student receives either in all their coursework or in a number of selected essays and projects.

8. Many first degree honours courses require students to write a dissertation, which is an extended essay on a subject of the student's choice (chosen in consultation with staff). Dissertations usually replace two or more examination papers.

Questions 1 to 5

Using information from the reading passage, complete the following sentences in NO MORE THAN THREE WORDS.

1 How long are Arts degrees in Scotland?

2 What is the name of courses which involve both normal study and practical job training?

3 How long is a full-time Higher National Diploma Course?

4 Which teaching method involves students discussing a subject they have already read about?

5 What kind of assessment is based on work done by the student during the course?

Check your answers with the Answer Key.

QUESTIONS ABOUT MAIN IDEAS

Questions about main ideas ask you to identify the main idea or topic of a section. There are two types of main idea questions: matching headings with paragraphs or sections, and identifying which sections relate to certain topics.

For both types of questions you should use the skill of skimming, but because the strategies are slightly different for each question type, we will look at them separately.

Main ideas: matching headings with paragraphs or sections

For these questions, each paragraph in the text needs a heading. Your task is to choose the correct one from the list of headings provided. In a question type like this, you should skim a paragraph or section before choosing the correct answer from the list. This is because when trying to match long pieces of text (e.g. paragraphs) to phrases (e.g. headings), it is more efficient to skim the long piece of text first. Then you can look through the alternative headings very quickly.

Step 1—Survey the text

Surveying has already been discussed several times in this book. Can you remember what to look at when you survey? Make a list, then check your answers with the section on surveying on pages 5–6.

In addition to surveying, remember that:

- the instructions may already have given you some useful information about the subject or source of the text
- if there is an introduction immediately after the title—as in the 'How to Revise for Exams' text—this can also give you some useful information to help you quickly understand what the rest of the text will be about.

Step 2—Skim read a paragraph

In most well-written English texts, every paragraph deals with a specific aspect of a topic. The first sentence of a paragraph usually tells the reader what the rest of the paragraph is about so when you are trying to identify the main idea of a paragraph, you should read the first sentence carefully. Then, keeping the idea of the first sentence in mind, you should quickly check the rest of the paragraph, picking up **only some** of the words. This kind of reading is called *skim reading* or *skimming*. Using this technique you will have a general idea of what the writer is saying about the topic.

Of course, when you skim read a text you cannot get as much information from the text as when you read it all carefully, but by skimming you can **quickly** get enough information to help you answer the question. Remember that efficient use of time is one of the most important exam skills. Look again at the Section 2 Demonstration questions 1–4, to remind you of how skimming works in practice.

You will have to adjust the speed of your skimming according to how easy the text is for you to understand. If a paragraph does not have a first sentence which gives the topic of the paragraph clearly, you have to skim more carefully. But don't forget that **you should not read every word**—reading every word will waste too much time.

Don't expect to be able to skim well immediately—you will have to practise. But most experts agree that it is a very important skill, not only for exams but also for all your future reading for study or work purposes.

ACTIVITY 13

The following text has questions which ask you to match headings with the paragraphs. Answer the questions, remembering to: survey the text, skim a paragraph/section for the main idea, and look for the correct heading from the list.

Time target: 5 minutes

Questions 1–5

Look at the text 'Difficulties Commonly Experienced by Overseas Students'.

There are six sections A–E.

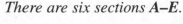

*Choose the most suitable heading for each section from the list of headings below. Write the appropriate numbers (**i–vi**) in the correct boxes on your answer sheet.*

Note: *There are more headings than sections so you will not use all of them. You may use any of the headings more than once.*

Example	Answer
Section A	**iv**

1	Section B	**4**	Section E
2	Section C	**5**	Section F
3	Section D		

List of headings

i   Personal Finances

ii   Language and Communication

iii Being Different and Apart

iv   Cultural Adjustment

v   Study-Related Concerns

vi   Family Support

vii Getting Around

viii Living Independently

DIFFICULTIES COMMONLY EXPERIENCED BY OVERSEAS STUDENTS

The problems experienced by overseas students are now generally well documented. The issues that cause the greatest difficulty can be summarised as follows:

A ....
This involves getting used to the new country and different way of life, customs, and values. In addition, students also have to deal with the sense of loss (missing family, friends, familiar food and places). These issues are usually referred to by the term 'culture shock'.

B ....
Managing on a limited budget is a challenge for most, but it is especially so for people living in an unfamiliar

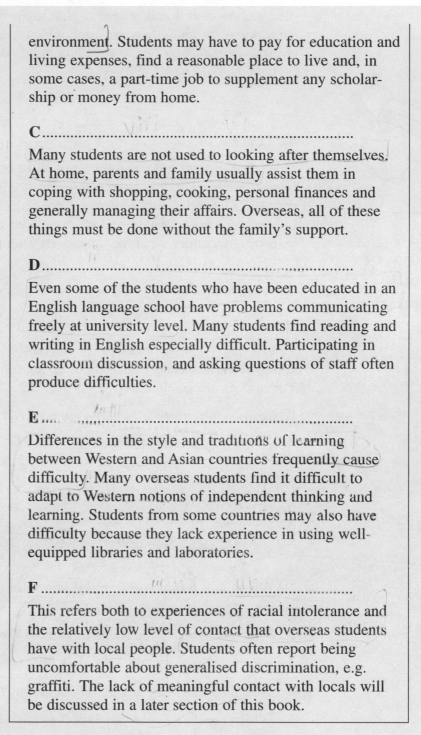

environment. Students may have to pay for education and living expenses, find a reasonable place to live and, in some cases, a part-time job to supplement any scholarship or money from home.

C ....

Many students are not used to looking after themselves. At home, parents and family usually assist them in coping with shopping, cooking, personal finances and generally managing their affairs. Overseas, all of these things must be done without the family's support.

D ....

Even some of the students who have been educated in an English language school have problems communicating freely at university level. Many students find reading and writing in English especially difficult. Participating in classroom discussion, and asking questions of staff often produce difficulties.

E ....

Differences in the style and traditions of learning between Western and Asian countries frequently cause difficulty. Many overseas students find it difficult to adapt to Western notions of independent thinking and learning. Students from some countries may also have difficulty because they lack experience in using well-equipped libraries and laboratories.

F ....

This refers both to experiences of racial intolerance and the relatively low level of contact that overseas students have with local people. Students often report being uncomfortable about generalised discrimination, e.g. graffiti. The lack of meaningful contact with locals will be discussed in a later section of this book.

Check your answers with the Answer Key.

Main ideas: identifying which sections relate to certain topics
The topic in each question needs to be matched with a paragraph or section of the reading text. This question type looks similar to the previous one but it requires a different strategy. It is better to read the question first to identify the topic, and then skim quickly through the text to find the

paragraph/section that is related to that topic. This is because there are only a few questions while there are a lot of paragraphs/sections. Therefore, many of the paragraphs/sections do not contain an answer, and you will waste your time if you try to look for one.

ACTIVITY 14

The following text consists of a set of short notices about a careers information program. It is an example of a text in which you cannot find the main idea in the first sentence. Consequently, you will have to skim a little more slowly. However, every notice has a heading, and these may help you to identify what the notices are about.

Time target: 6 minutes

Questions 1–5

The 'Industry Visit Workshops' notice on the next page has information about 10 guest speakers at a school giving information about their jobs. The notices are labelled **a–j.**

Write the appropriate letters (a–j) in boxes 1–5 on your answer sheet.

Note: *You may use any letter more than once.*

Example	*Answer*
Which talk would you attend if you wanted to work with children?	**b**

1 Which talk would you attend if you were interested in working in a department store?

2 Which talk would you attend to find out about working for a newspaper?

3 Which speaker will probably talk about charitable and social work?

4 Which speaker will talk about computing?

5 Which speaker would you expect to talk about the importance of personal appearance?

Check your answers with the Answer Key.

Careers Information Program

This term, 10 guest speakers will be coming to the school to talk about their jobs. The program is as follows:

a. Against the law Find out about the workings of a large inner-city legal firm. Find out how the support staff handle the complex workings of the court. Learn how to interpret the legalese used in legal documents.	**b. Growing concerns** This speaker will explain how local authority child-care services operate. Areas covered in the talk include pre-school and day-care facilities and activities.
c. Fast food The sick and the elderly often have difficulty feeding themselves. Meals on wheels is a non-profit making service which ensures that people who are unable to cook for themselves can eat well without having to leave their homes.	**d. Your very good health** Modern hospitals have many of the facilities of a 5-star hotel. Learn how today's doctors and nurses care not only for their patients' health, but also for their comfort.
e. The long and the short of it Hairdressing is a serious business that involves a wide variety of skills. Clients can have their hair cut, styled, dyed, tinted, permed or straightened. And that's just for starters! Learn all about the glamour and the glitter of the beauty business.	**f. Stop press** A story can break at any time so it's important that there's always someone on the job who can be on the spot within minutes to get the news out. And then there are the times when nothing much happens but there's still a paper to sell. Learn about the thrills and the frustrations of work on one of the biggest dailies.
g. Are you being served? From the art of arranging the window displays, to the science of stock control—the range of activities involved in the retail trade is enormous. This talk introduces you to the business of buying and selling to the general public.	**h. Comprehensive cover** Accidents happen. Things get stolen. People get sick, and eventually we all die. Insurance softens the shock of some of life's hard blows. Determining the risks is mostly done by computers and this speaker will explain the management of insurance data bases.

i. The hospitality industry	*j. Dr. Doolittle, I presume?*
From cooking to cleaning. From purchasing to delivering to the table. It all happens in a hotel. Find out about your job options in a five-star hotel.	Cats, dogs, birds and even goldfish catch a cold from time to time. And that's when you call for the vet. This busy little surgery will give you a thorough overview of animal health.

Summary—Section 2

There are usually two texts. Each text has only one type of question. Because the strategies for each type of question are different, the first thing you should do in Section 2 is **look at the questions to identify the question type.**

QUESTIONS ABOUT SPECIFIC INFORMATION

- Completing sentences
- True, False, Not Given
- Matching pieces of specific information
- Other question-types as in Section 1

Next, follow the three-step strategy to make finding the answer easier.

Step 1 Survey the text
- look at any parts of the text that stand out (e.g. the title, pictures, etc.)

Step 2 Read the instructions and the question
- make sure you know *how* you must answer the questions
- underline the key words

Step 3 Look for the answers
- scan for key words or synonyms by *looking over* the text
- do *not* read every word

QUESTIONS ABOUT MAIN IDEAS

Matching headings with paragraphs

Step 1 Survey the text

Step 2 Skim the paragraph to identify the topic
- the topic sentence is usually the first one in a paragraph
- skim the rest of the paragraph to make sure

Step 3 Choose the correct heading from the list

Identifying where to find information

Step 1 Survey the text

Step 2 Read the question to identify the topic
- underline the key words in the question
- read one question at a time

Step 3 Skim the paragraphs to find the one related to the topic
- the topic sentence is often the first one
- skim the rest of the paragraph quickly to confirm

Skills Focus

Guessing the Meaning of Words

While you are reading, you will probably find many words you do not understand. However, this does not have to be a problem. Firstly, you should decide whether the word is important for you. Understanding the word may not be necessary to answer the question. If you think the word is important, there are many strategies you can use to help you guess the meaning of a word.

Look at the context
Often you can guess the meaning of a word from the other words around it.

Check the part of speech of a word
Knowing whether the word is a noun (singular or plural), verb, adjective or an adverb can help you to decide on its meaning within the context. Also, you may already know one form of the word (e.g. the noun *nation*) but not the others (e.g. the adjective *national*, the noun *nationality*, or the verb *to nationalise*), so you should look closely at the root word to give you a clue.

Use your previous knowledge of English
You may have seen the word in a different context. You can use your previous knowledge and the new context to work out the meaning. Or you may know the separate parts of a word, but may be unfamiliar with the word as a whole. You can use this knowledge to help you work out the meaning.

Check if there is a definition
Sometimes there will be a definition, explanation or example of an unknown word. These can be introduced by a variety of words—*is, means, refers to, in other words,* and *i.e.*..

Look for any linking words or discourse markers
Linking words or discourse markers—such as *however, but, therefore, for example, so that, finally*—may help to indicate the meaning of a particular word.

Use your general background knowledge
Your knowledge and experience about what is logical or illogical can help you to guess the meaning of some words.

Demonstration — Examples

The following sentences are taken from the Section 1 text 'Your Post Office' on page 2.

1 More staff at <u>peak</u> periods for faster service.

Part of speech: normally a noun, but here acting as an adjective describing 'periods'.
Your knowledge of the root word: you may know that the noun 'peak' means the top or highest point on a mountain.
The context: you need to have more staff to give faster service during these times. Therefore, you can guess that 'peak periods' means periods with the highest or maximum number of customers, or the busiest periods.

2 New vending machine services such as cash-change machines, and phonecard and stamp <u>dispensers</u> for faster service.

Linking words: the words 'machine services such as...' tell you that a dispenser is a kind of machine.
The context: the text is talking about people obtaining (buying) things from machines. If people can serve themselves, the service should be faster.
You can guess that a dispenser is a kind of machine that sells or gives out things automatically.

3 <u>Extended</u> opening hours at selected main offices.

Part of speech: 'extended' is an adjective (i.e. past participle form) describing 'opening hours'.
Background knowledge: an adjective to describe 'opening hours' (the hours that the Post Office is open) can only be about *more* or *less* hours.
Context: The text is talking about providing a better service.
Knowledge of the root word: you may know that 'extend' means to make longer. So, you can guess that 'extended' must mean longer.

4 The tablets contain <u>doses</u> that are safe for children, so there's no danger of <u>overdose</u> ('Easy Riders', page 7.)

Part of speech: both words are nouns. The prefix *over-* means 'more' or 'too much'.
Context: the words 'tablets contain doses' tell you that a dose is something inside the tablet, or part of the ingredients. Also, this part of the text is talking about safety and danger. An overdose is negative (dangerous).
Background knowledge: a medicine can be dangerous if a person (especially a child) takes too much.
Therefore, you can guess that a dose is an amount of medicine in the tablet and an overdose is too much medicine.

5 ...we need about 50mg of vitamin C per day, and we can get it <u>readily</u> from citrus fruits, tomatoes and green vegetables. ('Sources of Vitamins', page 10.)

Part of speech: 'readily' is an adverb describing how we get vitamin C from those sources.

Context: the sentence is talking about being able to get our minimum requirement of vitamin C from the sources mentioned.
Background knowledge: you may know that these fruits and vegetables contain a lot of vitamin C. We can guess that 'readily' means 'easily' or 'in great quantity'.

6 Most vitamins we need are available in sufficient quantities in vegetables and fruits … Some vitamins, however, can only be found in <u>significant</u> quantities in animal products.

Part of speech: significant is an adjective describing the noun 'quantities'.
Context: the text is talking about how much a vitamin we can get from different sources. The first sentence says that we can get 'sufficient quantities' (enough) of most vitamins from vegetables and fruits.
Linking words: The word 'however' shows that the information in the second sentence contrasts with the information in the first sentence. The main contrast is between animal products and vegetables/fruits as different sources of vitamins. Therefore, you can guess that the meaning of 'significant quantities' is similar to the meaning of *sufficient* quantities.

ACTIVITY 15

For the examples below, try to work out the meaning of the <u>underlined</u> words using the strategies described above. Choose the correct answer **a, b or c.**

The following examples are taken from the reading 'The Coming Crisis in Long-Term Care' in Section 3 on pages 51–3.

1 While only 5 per cent of Americans over 65 currently <u>reside</u> in nursing homes, that percentage rises sharply with age. Twenty-two per cent of persons 85 and older live in nursing homes.

    a live

    b work

    c visit

2 According to national estimates, one year in a nursing home costs an average of $22 000, and this is expected to more than double by 2018. Given that the mean income for Americans aged 65 and older is currently $19 000, nursing home care would <u>exhaust</u> the assets and available income of most elderly people in just one year.

    a tire out

    b use up completely

    c pay for

3 But how will such insurance be funded —publicly or privately? While some groups urge a publicly funded program, there are <u>grave</u> doubts about the willingness of taxpayers to pay for a public program.

    a very few

    b serious

    c no

4 The federal government already faces a budget <u>deficit</u>, which threatens cutbacks in existing programs. The substantial extra expenditure of a publicly funded program would certainly lose votes.

    a profit

    b stability

    c loss

5 Individuals would thus still be responsible for <u>footing</u> the bill for their own long-term care.

    a paying

    b counting

    c writing

Section 3

Step One	Survey the text
Step Two	Skim the text to identify its organisation
Step Three	Read the question
Step Four	Skim or scan for the answer

In this section there is only one longer reading text (about 700 words), usually without subheadings. There will be three or four different types of questions. The question-types could be:

- any of those from Sections 1 or 2
- completing a summary
- completing a table
- identifying qualities or characteristics.

Because the text is quite long, and because you will be looking for different kinds of information, it is a good idea to first **survey the text** to identify the topic, and then **skim the text to identify how the information is organised** before you start answering the questions.

As with Section 2 of the test, the skills of scanning and skimming are very important in this section. You must use your time efficiently. The following Demonstration section will show you how to answer the questions without wasting time. Skills and strategies will be discussed in the *Analysis and Practice* section which follows the Demonstration.

Do not read the demonstration text and questions first. Go directly to the *How to Answer* section on page 47, and refer back to the reading text as instructed.

Demonstration—Text and Questions

Questions 1–4

The passage has 8 paragraphs labelled **A–H**.

Which paragraphs contain the following information?

*Write the appropriate letters **A–H** in boxes 1–4 on your answer sheet.*
*You only need **ONE** letter for each answer.*

Note: *You may use each letter more than once.*

Example	*Answer*
Numbers living in cities between 1950 and 1985.	**A**

1 The number of large cities in Africa.

2 The projected population of Mexico City.

3 An explanation of what 'natural' population increase is.

4 The lack of clean water in cities.

 URBANISATION

A The *United Nations Human Development Report 1990* has called this 'the century of the great urban explosion'. Between 1950 and 1985 the number of people living in cities in the world nearly tripled. In the developing world, it quadrupled—from less than 300 million to about 1.2 billion. In Africa, the population of the larger cities increased more than sevenfold over this period.

B Although the rate of city growth is expected to slow in the future, the absolute numbers added each year will continue to grow. Most of this growth—as much as two-thirds in many Asian and Latin American cities—will come from natural increase (i.e. the excess of births over deaths) of populations already in cities. The rest will come from rural-urban migration (in part a result of high rural fertility putting pressure on agricultural livelihoods) and the urbanisation of currently rural areas.

C In future, the urban population of the developing countries is expected to grow by nearly another billion in the next fifteen years. By 2015, half the developing world's people will live in urban areas. Growth rates will be fastest in Africa, though absolute growth will be greatest in Asia, where cities will gain 500 million inhabitants between 1985 and the turn of the century.

D An increasing proportion of the urbanised population will be living in huge cities. The number of cities with a million or more inhabitants in developing countries was only 28 in 1950. By 1989 there were 125, and there will be a projected 277 in the year 2000. Africa had only one such city in 1950. By 2000 Africa could have 60 cities of a million or more.

E However, urban growth in developing countries has not been evenly distributed between all cities. In most countries one or two giant cities have grown out of all proportion, cornering the lion's share of investment, industry and government spending—but also creating problems of congestion, squalor and unrest.

F In 1970, only 13 per cent of the urban population of developing countries lived in cities with more than four million people. By 2025, such cities are expected to house 28 per cent of town dwellers. While many northern cities such as London or Paris have levelled out or reduced their populations, the dominant cities of developing countries have grown exponentially. The populations of Tehran, Karachi and Manila grew at 5 per cent or more a year in the 1970s, and those of Delhi, Mexico City, Seoul, Sao Paolo and Jakarta at between 4 and 5 per cent. A number of cities may grow to gigantic size. Mexico City, which had a population of 15 million in 1980, may grow to nearly 25 million by the year 2000. Greater <u>Bombay</u>, which had only 3 million inhabitants in 1950, is expected to be the second largest with over 15 million. Jakarta will be third, with an estimated 13 million or more inhabitants by the turn of the century.

G While the balanced, gradual growth of cities of half a million or less is rarely a problem, rapid urbanisation, especially in poor countries, nearly always is. The growth of urban populations has regularly outpaced the growth of paying jobs and of government resources for infrastructure and services, such as sewerage and water supply. Large proportions of urban dwellers live in illegal, self-built housing without secure tenure or facilities. An estimated 40 per cent live in such conditions in Nairobi, Lima and Manila, and around 60 per cent in Delhi and El Salvador. One city dweller in three had no access to clean water in 1983, and two out of three had no proper sanitation. Some make their homes—and their livings—on rubbish dumps.

H In dealing with problems like this, attention must be focused not only on cities. City dwellers do need cheap land and building materials, secure tenure and local employment. More attention also needs to be given to reversing appalling urban environmental deterioration. But improving conditions in rural areas will also help. People in country areas would then have much less incentive to migrate to cities. Any measure that leads to a slowing down in the rate of urban population growth will contribute to an improvement of living conditions there.

Complete the table below using **A NUMBER, OR NO MORE THAN THREE WORDS**. Write your answers in boxes 5–9 on your answer sheet.

When	Where	What
1950–2000	Greater Bombay	*Example* an increase of more than **12 million** inhabitants
.....(5).....	developing countries	half of the people will be living in cities
1950–1985	.....(6).....	the number of people living in cities increased by 3 times
2000	.....(7).....	will be the city with the third largest population
1985–2000	Asia	the number of people living in cities will grow by .....(8).....
.....(9).....	various cities in developing countries	a large percentage of people living in illegal housing

Questions 10–13

The following is a brief summary of part of the reading passage. Complete each gap in the summary by choosing a word from the box.

Note: There are more words than gaps so you will not need to use them all. You may use any word more than once.

Summary

Example

Urban growth is a **problem** when it is faster than the growth in jobs and essential services.

Many people living in .....(10)..... have inadequate housing without sanitation or clean water supplies. There are two main ways of addressing these problems. The first is to improve conditions in cities, for example by providing cheaper, more secure housing and improving urban .....(11)..... . The second is to spend more money on .....(12)..... development, thereby .....(13)..... the rates of migration from rural to urban areas.

developing countries	problem	housing
reducing	urban	rural
cities	growing	expensive
environments	increase	

How to Answer

In this section, we show you how to answer only *some* of the Demonstration questions. At the end of Section 3 we will ask you to answer the remaining questions, using the skills and strategies that you learn and practise in the following pages.

STEP 1—SURVEY THE TEXT

The title of the extract, 'Urbanisation', tells you (if you know the word) that the text is about the growth or development of cities. There are 8 paragraphs labelled A–H. No other information is available from quickly surveying the text, so to find out about what aspect of urbanisation is discussed in the text, you will have to go on to step 2.

STEP 2—SKIM THE TEXT TO IDENTIFY ITS ORGANISATION

Paragraph A introduces the idea of cities growing fast, especially in developing countries.

Paragraph B deals with the *future* growth of cities. By reading only those words in black print in the remainder of the paragraph we see that reasons are given for this growth.

Paragraph C gives some details of the size of future growth. If you read only the words in black print in the rest of the paragraph, you can see that the paragraph goes on to talk about the 'fastest' growth, in Africa and Asia.

Paragraph D mentions 'huge cities'. The rest of the paragraph gives details about the past and future growth of very big cities.

Paragraph E introduces the idea of uneven growth of cities in developing countries. The rest of the paragraph talks about the problems of the 'giant' cities.

Paragraph F introduces the topic of cities which have a population of over 4 million. The rest of the paragraph lists some of these 'giant' cities and gives details of their size and growth rates.

Paragraph G touches on the problems of these very large cities in poor countries. The paragraph continues to give examples of some of the problems.

Paragraph H starts to talk about solutions to the problems mentioned earlier in the text. The remainder of the paragraph states what these solutions are.

From skimming the text we know how the text is organised. The organisation of the text can be summarised as follows:

Paragraph	Main topic
A	An introduction to urban growth and some statistics of past growth
B	Causes of continued growth in developing countries
C	Future growth statistics in developing countries
D	Increase in the number of large cities in the developing world
E	The (uneven) nature of urban growth, including some problems
F	Examples of giant cities in developing countries
G	Problems caused by the fast growth of cities
H	Suggested solutions

QUESTION 1

Step 3—Read the question
You are looking for the location of pieces of specific information. You have to indicate the location by choosing only **one** paragraph. (Notice that the key words in the sentence are underlined.)

The number of large cities in Africa.

Step 4—Look for the answer
From your knowledge of the organisation of the text, you can guess that this information might be in paragraphs A, C or D.

Scanning for the key word 'Africa', you see that the sentence with this word in paragraph A says nothing about numbers of cities. The same is true of paragraph C. In paragraph D, the last two sentences mention 'Africa'. Here the text gives numbers of cities, so **D** is the correct answer.

QUESTION 2

Step 3—Read the question

The projected population of Mexico in the year 2000.

Step 4—Find the answer
It is difficult to predict the location of this information. Paragraphs A, C, D or F could give details of the population of a large city like Mexico. However, it will be relatively easy to scan for the name of the city.

Mexico City is mentioned twice in paragraph F. The second time gives the predicted future population—**F** is the correct answer.

QUESTIONS 3 AND 4

These questions are not answered here. At the end of Section 3 you will be asked to answer them, using the skills and strategies that you will learn later in this section.

QUESTION 5

Step 3—Read the question

The instructions tell you to fill in the numbered gaps in the table with *a number or one, two or three (but no more) words*.

Before trying to answer questions 5–9, it is important to be able to read the table. Move your eyes across the table to get an idea of how it is organised. There are three types of information included: *when, where* and *what*. To see what kind of answer is needed for question 5, read across the table: *where?* 'in developing countries'; *what?* 'half the population will be living in cities'. The missing information is the answer to the question *when?*

Changing the gap in the table to a question you get:

<u>When will</u> half of the populations of developing countries be living in cities?

The word 'will' indicates that you must look for a time (a year) in the future.

Step 4—Find the answer

From the initial skim reading of the text, you can guess that this information will be in either paragraphs A, C, or D.

By scanning paragraph A you will not find a future time reference. Paragraph C mentions the year 2015 in the second half of the first sentence. Reading this sentence confirms that it talks about the specific information mentioned in the question—**2015** is the correct answer.

QUESTION 6

Step 3—Read the question

Use the information in the *where* and *what* columns to clarify the question:

<u>Where</u> did the number of people living in cities increase by about 3 times between 1950 and 1985?

Step 4—Find the answer

This information could be in paragraphs A, D or F. Scanning for the years 1950 and 1985—numbers are always easier to scan for than words—in paragraph A, you find both of them in the second half of the first sentence. Three statistics are given for this time period, regarding the number of people living in cities.

1   '… in the world nearly tripled' (tripled = 3 times)
2   'In the developing world … quadrupled' (quadrupled = four times)
3   'In Africa (larger cities) … increased more than sevenfold' (sevenfold = 7 times)

So the correct answer is **the world**. (If you did not know what the word 'tripled' means, the word 'nearly' could help you to choose the correct answer. In this context, 'nearly' has a similar meaning to the word which is used in the question, 'about'.

QUESTIONS 7–9

These questions are not answered here. At the end of Section 3 you will be asked to answer them, using the skills and strategies that you learn later.

QUESTIONS 10–13

Step 3—Read the question

You are instructed to complete the **summary** of **part** of the text by choosing words from the box. But which part of the text does it summarise? Briefly skim the whole summary. The first half of the summary talks about the problems of urban growth, and the second half talks about the solutions. You already know that paragraph G deals with the problems, and that paragraph H deals with the solutions, so it is reasonably clear that the summary deals with **the last two paragraphs** of the text.

QUESTION 10

Step 3—Read the question

> Many people living in .....*(10)*..... have inadequate housing without sanitation or clean water supplies.

Step 4—Find the answer

Looking at the first sentence you can see that you need a **noun** to fill the gap. If you scan the words in the box you can eliminate the words *reducing, urban, rural, growing* and *expensive*. Scanning paragraph G for 'inadequate housing' or synonyms, you find 'live in illegal, self-built housing without secure tenure or facilities'. The subject of the verb *live* is 'large proportions of urban dwellers', so you are looking for a word which means 'urban' but is a noun. Look at the box again and you will find the word **cities**. This is the correct answer.

QUESTION 11

Step 3—Read the question

> The first is to improve conditions in cities, for example by providing cheaper, more secure housing and improving urban .....*(11)*..... .

Step 4—Find the answer

Looking at the sentence you can see that you need a **noun** which can be described by *urban*. If you scan the words in the box you can eliminate *reducing, urban, rural, growing, expensive* and *cities*. Looking back at the summary sentence you will see that the first example of improving urban conditions is 'cheaper, more secure housing'. You need to find *another* example, so it is also unlikely that the answer is *housing*.

Now scan paragraph H. The second sentence in that paragraph mentions four solutions to improve conditions in cities—land, materials, tenure and employment. The first three are covered by the words 'cheaper, more secure housing' in the summary, and the fourth solution, employment, is not mentioned in the choices in the box. Therefore you must go on to the third sentence in paragraph H, which talks about 'reversing appalling environmental deterioration'. If you look in the box for a noun form of 'environmental' or its synonym, you will find the word **environments**. This is the answer.

QUESTIONS 12—13

These questions are not answered here. At the end of Section 3 you will be asked to answer them, using the skills and strategies that you learn later.

Analysis and Practice

As with Section 2 of the test, in Section 3 there are main idea questions and questions for specific information. Skimming and scanning are very useful. You will probably find these skills difficult to acquire, initially, but with continued practice you will see more clearly how useful they are.

To read any complete text carefully takes time so remember that to answer questions about a text you only need to read **parts** of the text carefully. Skimming and scanning will help you find those important parts of the text so you will not waste time on irrelevant parts of the text.

ACTIVITY 16

In the following text some of the words have been printed in black. These are an example of the words you might read while skimming to identify the organisation of the text. Read only the words in black print and then try to complete the table of the main topics of the various paragraphs below.

Time target: 4 minutes

The Coming Crisis In Long-Term Care

1 The greying of America has many health-care planners worried. The life expectancies of even the very old (85 and older) have increased significantly in recent years, but at the same time, this group faces the highest risk of chronic disease and disability requiring long-term care. Paying for this care could wipe out the entire life savings of many people within a year.

2 The number of Americans aged 85 and older is expected to grow three to four times as fast as the general population between 1990 and 2010 and is expected to increase from 2 million in 1980 to 16 million by the year 2050. Of major significance for long-term care are the lengthening life expectancies at age 85, which have increased 24% since 1960 and are projected to increase another 44% by 2040.

3 While only 5% of Americans over 65 currently reside in nursing homes, that percentage rises sharply with age.

Twenty-two per cent of persons 85 and older live in nursing homes.

4   According to national estimates, one year in a nursing home costs an average of $22 000, and this figure is expected to more than double by 2018. Given that the mean income for Americans aged 65 and older is currently $19 000, most people in that age group will simply not be able to stay in nursing homes.

5   Long-term care is costly even when provided in the home. One study found that more than 60% of elderly people living alone and 40% of elderly couples would become impoverished after one year of seven-days-a-week care.

6   Many people still mistakenly believe that Medicare covers long-term chronic care, the report says. But Medicare typically covers hospital and physicians' costs for acute illnesses or injuries and covers nursing-home stays of no more than 150 days. Awareness of Medicare's limitations is growing, however, and more people now see some form of long-term care insurance as desirable to protect against financial ruin.

7   But how will such insurance be funded—publicly or privately? While some groups urge a publicly funded program, there are grave doubts about the willingness of taxpayers to pay for a public program. The federal government already faces a budget deficit, which threatens cutbacks in existing programs. The substantial extra expenditure of a publicly funded program would certainly lose votes.

8   Two possible routes for private insurance plans are individual plans and employer-sponsored plans. Individual policies covering long-term care are currently the most widely available coverage. In 1983, only 16 companies offered individual long-term care policies. In 1988, there were more than 100. By 1987, about 400 000 people owned long-term care insurance policies; in 1988, there were more than 1 million. However, these are mostly younger workers. The number of those over 65 with such policies today is still relatively small, at approximately 100 000.

9   Employer-sponsored plans are, however, gaining acceptance especially when offered as part of a flexible, or 'cafeteria', benefits program.

10 Providing for long-term care insurance through employer groups can help lower plan costs by spreading

the long-term care risk over a larger risk pool and through concurrent savings in administrative costs. Another **advantage** of employer-sponsored plans over individual policies is that they **encourage younger workers to** enter the program. The younger the participant is at the time of entering the program, **the lower are his or her premium rates.** Successful plans would also have an **inflation-protection** feature.

11   Employer-sponsored programs are unlikely to be paid entirely—or even partly—by employers. Rather, **employee-pay-all plans** are the most likely scenario, given the rising employer costs for the employer-paid benefit plans already in effect.

12   Individuals would thus still be responsible for footing the bill for their own long-term care. But by planning well ahead of time and entering early in an employer-sponsored insurance plan, an individual may pay as little as $20 a month in premium.

Paragraph	Main topic
1	The nature of the crisis
2 and 3	Statistics on the growing numbers of elderly people
4 and 5	
6	
7	
8	
9,10 and 11	
12	

Check your answers in the Answer Key.

COMPLETING A TABLE

The first activity related to this text is *completing a table*. These are simply questions for specific information in another form. It may help you to convert the space in the table into a question in the usual form. For an example see questions 5–9 in the Demonstration for Section 3.

ACTIVITY 17

By filling in the above table you know something about the organisation of 'The Coming Crisis in Long-Term Care', and where you might find certain information. Reread the <u>entire</u> text then answer questions 1–4. Use your knowledge of the text and scan for key words or numbers. Don't forget to survey the table to understand its organisation before you begin to look for the answers.

Time target: 3–4 minutes

Questions 1–4

Complete the table below which gives information about two age categories mentioned in the reading passage. Write A NUMBER in the correct boxes on your answer sheet.

	Age group 65 and over	Age group 85 and over
percentage living in nursing homes	.....(1).....per cent	.....(2).....per cent
expected total number in 2050		e.g. **16 million**
current average income	.....(3).....dollars	
number having long-term-care insurance policies	.....(4).....	

Check your answers in the Answer Key.

MATCHING A QUALITY OR A CHARACTERISTIC

In the next activity, there is another question type for the same text, namely *matching a quality or characteristic to a subject*. This type of question requires you to look for specific information. To answer the questions efficiently, you should use your knowledge of the organisation of the text and, using key words, scan for the specific information needed.

ACTIVITY 18

Time target: 3 minutes

Questions 1–4

Look at the features of different insurance schemes listed. State which scheme has these characteristics.

In boxes 1–4 on your answer sheet write:

    I   *if it applies to individually funded schemes*

    M   *if it applies to Medicare*

    P   *if it applies to other publicly funded schemes*

    E   *if it applies to employer-sponsored schemes*

1 currently the most popular long-term scheme

2 does not provide long-term nursing care

3 is unlikely because it is politically unpopular

4 reduces the costs by insuring in work-related groups

Check your answers in the Answer Key.

ACTIVITY 19

Survey and skim the next extract, 'Killer Robots'. Then complete the chart following the text to show that you have identified the organisation of the text. You should be able to complete the chart quickly by skimming. Do not waste time reading the text carefully.

Time target: 4 minutes

 Killer Robots

Rules for working safely

A Robots are taking over many hazardous jobs, but they are also creating new hazards, according to a report by the International Labour Office (ILO).

B Being struck by a robot arm in motion, being trapped between the robot and another object, and being hit by an object dropped by an overloaded robot gripper are the main hazards that robots pose to humans, according to the report, *Safety in the Use of Industrial Robots*. In many cases, workers are in the way when the robot makes a sudden, unexpected movement or starts when it isn't supposed to. Such miscues may result from software problems, electrical interference, or faults in the hydraulic, electrical, or pneumatic controls.

C The first robot-related death occurred in Japan in 1981, and one survey of robot use in Japan showed a total of 10 fatalities reported by the end of April 1987. The causes were the victim's error in four cases and 'spontaneous start of robot' in the other six, according to Japan's Ministry of Labour. Each year, approximately five or six workers are injured in robot accidents in Japan, and there have been many more 'near-misses'. But, as the ILO points out, more than 100 000 robots are used in Japanese factories.

D In the United States as well, control problems account for a large share of injuries to workers, but one fatality described in the report was the result of a worker simply ignoring safety precautions and attempting to clean up an area where a robot was operating.

E Even when robots are used safely, other problems may develop, says the report. When robots create unemployment of humans, workers may suffer from ulcers, colitis, and emotional stress. New jobs created by robotisation generate stress, too, such as anxiety in trying to keep pace with a robot's work pace.

F 'In general, while technological innovation may free people from physical labour, it may give rise to mental load,' the report notes, 'and it is thought likely that new occupational diseases may arise in time. The development of a special curriculum, in Japan known as robot medicine, acknowledges the connection between emerging technology and stress.'

G The report cites several rules for robot workers that may help prevent future injuries. For example, robots should be easy to operate. Robots should also be designed so that in the event of a breakdown, they can only harm themselves and not humans. In addition, robots should leave an area after finishing their task so that they do not interfere with other workers—human or robotic.

H The report also mentions rules that will help reduce robot-related anxieties. Robots must not replace people in desirable jobs but only jobs people do not wish to do or find dangerous. Also, robots must obey humans so that they do not psychologically or physically oppress people. Finally, if robots replace humans on a job, the people affected must give their approval.

Paragraph	Main topic
A	Introduction
B	The ways that injuries happen
C	
D	

| E and F |
| G |
| H |

Check your answers in the Answer Key.

In the next activity, there are three question types for the text you have just read.

Questions 1–4 Identifying which paragraph contains certain information (see the Section 3 Demonstration). Scan for key words, names or numbers using your knowledge of the organisation of the text.

Questions 5–6 Identifying a number of qualities or characteristics from a list—in this case two causes of something. This is a question for specific information. It is easier to find the relevant information about the causes first, and then compare that information against the list to find the correct answers. Do not waste time looking in the text for items on the list—many of them will not be mentioned in the text.

Questions 7–8 Completing a statement in no more than three words (see Section 2) These are questions for specific information. Use your knowledge of the organisation of the text and scan for key words.

ACTIVITY 20

From your skim reading, you already know something about the organisation of the text. While you are answering the questions, try to concentrate only on those parts of the texts where you think the answers might be found.

Time target: 10 minutes

Questions 1–4

The passage 'Killer Robots' has 8 paragraphs labelled A–H.

Which paragraphs contain the following information?

*Write the appropriate letters **A–H** in the correct boxes on your answer sheet. You need only one letter for each answer.*

Note: *You may use each letter more than once.*

Example	Answer
Description of an incident in the United States	**D**

1 The most common ways that robots cause physical injuries.

2 Regulations to prevent stress-related problems.

3 The names of illnesses caused by the psychological effects of robots on workers.

4 The number of physical injuries which occur.

Questions 5–6

The reading passage gives two main causes of mental stress from robots. Identify these two causes by choosing two items from the list below.

*Write the appropriate number (**i–v**) in the correct boxes on your answer sheet. The order is not important.*

i   robots are difficult to operate   *ii   robots work too fast*

iii   robots injure workers' friends   *iv   people lose their jobs to robots*

v   robots make sudden unexpected movements

Questions 7–8

*Complete the following statements in **NO MORE THAN THREE WORDS**. Write your answers in the correct boxes on your answer sheet.*

7 The reading passage is based on information from the

_____

8 To prevent physical injury, robots which have completed the job they were working on should

_____

Check your answers with the Answer Key.

SUMMARY GAP-FILL

The final question type involves choosing the correct word or group of words to fill in sentence gaps in a summary of the text. (For an example, see the Section 3 Demonstration questions 10–13.)

For summary gap-fill questions, you should practise the following steps.

Step 1   Identify whether the summary applies to all or only part of the text. If it covers only part, you will have to find which part. The easiest way to do this is to read the beginning of the summary and match that information with the text itself.

Step 2   Read from the beginning of the summary up to and including a sentence with a gap.

Step 3   Go to the relevant part of the text. Skim or scan for the answer. Check the choices in the box to find the word from the text or a synonym.

Step 4 If you are unsure of your answer, identify the part of speech (noun, verb, adjective, adverb) of the word needed to fill the gap. Then look again at the choices in the box. You can immediately eliminate some of the choices because they are the wrong part of speech.

Step 5 Go back to the summary and read up to and including the next sentence with a gap, and so on.

ACTIVITY 21

The following activity contains some summary gap-fill questions for the 'Killer Robots' text. Answer the questions by following the steps noted above.

Time target: 6 minutes

Questions 1–6

Complete the summary of the reading passage. Choose your answers from the box following the summary and write them in the correct boxes on your answer sheet.

Note: *There are more words than spaces so you will not need to use them all. You may use any word more than once.*

Summary

.....(1)..... the benefits of using industrial robots, there are two main problems which can arise. Firstly, although some robot-related injuries can be said to be caused by the .....(2)..... , robots themselves sometimes cause physical injury or even .....(3)..... because of various hardware and software faults. Secondly, robots create various .....(4)..... problems in humans. These are being addressed by a new field of study called robot-medicine.

.....(5)..... prevent both of these kinds of problems, various .....(6)..... about the design of robots and their use and application should be observed.

over-loaded	rules	despite
due to	in order to	death
hazardous	hazards	workers
stress-related	so	

ACTIVITY 22

The Demonstration text in Section 3—'Urbanisation'—discussed the growth of cities and resulting problems. Not all of the text questions were answered in the Demonstration so should now answer the remaining questions—questions 3–4, 7–9, and 12–13. Go through all of the necessary steps. You will have to survey the text again and skim it to identify its organisation before you begin answering the questions.

Time target: 10 minutes

Check your answers with the Answer Key.

Summary—Section 3

Section 3 of the test has one longer reading text with up to four different question types.

QUESTION TYPES

- any question type from Sections 1 and 2
- completing a table
- identifying qualities or characteristics from a list
- completing a summary.

STRATEGIES

Skimming—looking quickly through a text and reading only some of the words in order to get a general idea about the topic or main idea.
Scanning—looking quickly for key words or synonyms.

To make finding the answer easier remember to follow these steps:
Step 1 Survey the text
- look at any parts of the text which stand out i.e. titles, headings, pictures etc.

Step 2 Skim the text to identify its organisation
- the topic is usually found in the first sentence
- skim the rest of the paragraph to confirm the topic

Step 3 Read the instructions and the question
- identify the question type
- underline key words in the instructions and the question

Step 4 Skim and/or scan for the answer
- **do not** read every word in the text. Step 2 will help you find information in the text quickly and efficiently.

Use the appropriate strategy according to the question type.

Skills Focus

Linking Words

Knowing the meaning and the purpose of linking words in sentences can be very useful for both the Reading and the Writing tests. The more common linking words can be divided into six main groups according to their purpose. (The following example sentences have all been taken from the reading 'Killer Robots' in Section 3.)

Showing sequence
    Finally, if robots replace humans on a job …

Giving additional information

In the United States <u>as well</u>, …

Giving examples

<u>For example,</u> robots should be easy to operate.

Expressing consequence or result

… robots should leave an area after finishing their task <u>so that</u> they do not interfere with other workers.

Giving reasons or causes

<u>The causes </u>were the victim's error in four cases …

… one fatality described in the report <u>was the result of</u> a worker simply ignoring safety precautions …

Showing contrast

Robots are taking over many hazardous jobs, <u>but</u> they are also creating new hazards …

ACTIVITY 23

Put the words in the box below into the correct group in the table.

even	be caused by this	however	after this
consequently	because	next	though
although	also	besides this	therefore
firstly	on the other hand	whereas	for instance
such as	because of this	even though	secondly
despite	and	in addition	then
result from	as well as	as a result	due to this
while	so	since	

Sequence	Addition	Example
finally	as well	for example

Reason/Cause	Consequence/Result	Contrast
the cause be the result of	so that	but

Note: Even though the above linking words may be in one group, they are often used in different ways in sentences. Check your dictionary or grammar book for examples of how to use these words in grammatically correct ways.

Students' Questions Answered

The Reading Test

Are question types limited to one section in the Reading test?	No, they aren't. However, you will usually find summary gap-fills in Section 3 only.
Can I ask the invigilator questions?	The invigilator is not allowed to answer any questions to help you understand the Reading test.
Can I write on the question paper?	Yes.
Can I change my answer after I've written it on the answer sheet?	Yes.
Can I use a pen?	No, you must use a pencil.
Can I use typex/correction fluid ?	No, you may only use an eraser or cross your answer out.
Are there penalties for the wrong answers in the Reading test ?	No, there aren't. If you are not sure of an answer, you should guess.
Should I answer the questions in sequence, i.e. Section 1, then 2, then 3?	It is a good idea because the texts get progressively longer and the questions more difficult.

Should I write the answers in the question booklet first and transfer them to the answer sheet at the end?	No, this is a complete waste of time.
How long should I spend on each question?	There are 40 questions in the test and you have an hour, so you have an average of 1.5 minutes per question. Therefore you should spend approximately 20 minutes on each section.
Why does it waste time if you read the text first and then answer the questions?	You will never have to read **every** word of any text to answer the questions. Your aim is to answer the questions, so you should practise scanning and skimming in order to locate the answers as quickly as possible.
If there are only 10 minutes left but I still have 10 questions to answer, what should I do?	You should continue answering the questions using the appropriate strategies, but if you really run out of time you should guess.
What should I do if I can't find the answer to one of the questions in the Reading test?	Don't waste lots of time looking for the answer to one question. Keep an eye on the time. If necessary, leave it and come back to it later. If you still can't find it then, guess.
Is it important to spell answers correctly?	If the spelling errors are serious your answer may be marked incorrect.
Does the answer have to be grammatically accurate in the 'complete with up to 3 words' questions?	There are 2 types of these questions. When you have to 'complete a sentence' the answer should be grammatically correct. However, when you have to 'answer a question' in no more than 3 words the answer does not have to be a complete, grammatically correct sentence.
When I write short answers, I often use words from the text. Do I have to always use the same word form as the word in the text?	No, not always. You will sometimes have to change the form of some words—from nouns to adjectives, from verbs to gerunds, and so on.
If the instruction says to write a letter of the alphabet on the answer sheet, but instead I write the answer in full, is that all right?	The answer will probably be marked wrong.
What is the difference between a statement that is FALSE and NOT GIVEN?	If an answer is FALSE, you must be able to find that the **opposite** is true somewhere in the text. If there is **no complete** information about something then it is NOT GIVEN.

Is it possible to answer a question with TRUE or FALSE if the answer is only implied and not specifically written ?	No, it must be stated, although it might not necessarily be in the same words.
How do I improve my reading ?	By reading more often—including a greater variety of texts, brochures, posters, etc.—and by practising the various skills described in this book.
How do I interpret my scores ?	Since the tests are scaled according their level of difficulty, you cannot say that 50% = Band 5. However you can use that as a **rough** guide. So if you are regularly getting 75% of the questions right, you are doing well.
Will the time be announced during the test?	Yes. The invigilators are supposed to give various time warnings during the test.

IELTS PRACTICE TEST

GENERAL TRAINING READING
TEST 1

TIME ALLOWED: 1 hour

NUMBER OF QUESTIONS: 40

Instructions

All answers must be written on the answer sheet

The test is divided as follows:

Section 1	Questions 1–12
Section 2	Questions 13–25
Section 3	Questions 26–40

Start at the beginning of the test and work through it. You should answer all questions.

If you cannot do a particular question, leave it and go on to the next. You can return to it later.

SECTION 1   *Questions 1–12*

Questions 1–5

Look at the advertisement for cheap theatre tickets. Match the information about the service with questions A–F in the picture.

*Write the appropriate letters **A–F** in boxes 1–5 on your answer sheet.*

Example

Cheap-Tix staff are theatre lovers too. They see almost every show in town and can give advice on a show to suit your requirements. Tourist maps and brochures are also available at the Cheap-Tix booth.

Answer **A**

1 In a word .... 'cash'. Credit cards, cheques or travellers' cheques are not accepted.

2 Tickets available to shows all over town are collected each morning from theatre box offices and ticket agencies and are offered for sale from 10 a.m. at the Cheap-Tix booth in the city mall.

3 Cheap-Tix does not offer advance bookings or sales information. Customers must come in person to the Cheap-Tix booth on the day of performance. Shows available are listed on the bulletin boards. There is no direct telephone link with the Cheap-Tix sales booth.

4 Anyone who goes to the Cheap-Tix booth can buy whatever tickets are available, making the service ideal for groups.

5 Cheap-Tix will sell tickets to any show it can get. This includes rock concerts and musicals.

Questions 6–9

Read the following advice about preventing tetanus.

Do the statements that follow agree with the information given in the text ?

In the boxes 6–9 on your answer sheet write:

TRUE   *if the statement is true*

FALSE   *if the statement is false*

NOT GIVEN   *if the information is not given in the passage*

Tetanus Injection

All wounds carry a risk of infection. Dirty wounds in particular carry a risk of tetanus infection. The bacteria that cause tetanus are present in the soil and in animal faeces. If they get into a wound they multiply very rapidly. Tetanus is a serious, potentially fatal condition. It can cause muscle spasms and leads to lockjaw. It can be prevented by a tetanus injection.

Have regular tetanus injections. A booster is recommended every five years. Always check that you are covered after any injury where the skin is broken.

Be particularly sure that children have regular tetanus injections. They are more prone to falling over and getting dirt in a wound than adults.

---

6 Tetanus can kill you.

7 Household pets should be given tetanus injections.

8 A single tetanus injection provides permanent protection.

9 Children have a higher risk than adults of getting tetanus.

Questions 10–12

*Read the following advertisements and answer the questions. Choose the appropriate letters **A–D** and write them in boxes 10–12 on your answer sheet.*

VISITING MELBOURNE?

Pick up a copy of *This Week in Melbourne*

It's full of up-to-the-minute information on:

- sightseeing

- shopping

- antiques and galleries

- wineries

- entertainment

- dining out and accommodation

Copies are available from the Victorian Government Travel Centre, 10 Jones Street, Sydney.

---

10   What is being advertised?

A   a hotel

B   a guided tour

C   a shopping mall

D   a tourist magazine

Photocopy cards

The college has introduced a new card system for obtaining photocopies called COPYCARD which replaces the old system. The most important feature of the new card system is card reusability. When you have used up all the credits on your card, you simply recharge it.

To get your COPYCARD:

1. go to the Students' Union office. When you have used the current credit in the card, simply return the card along with a cash payment for the amount of credit you want added, or

2. there is a card dispenser in the library.

There is a unit cost of $1.50 per card.

If you have any further enquiries you can contact the Technical Officer at the Students' Union.

Questions 11 and 12

11 The old cards

A were cheaper   B   were not reliable

C could not be used again   D   cost $1.50

12 When your card has run out of credits

A you can decide how many more credits you want to buy

B you have to pay $1.50

C you should contact the Technical Officer

D you will have to buy a new one

SECTION 2   *Questions 13–25*

Questions 13–18

Look at the welcome letter to students.

The text has 7 sections (1–7).

Choose the most suitable heading for each section from the list of headings below.

*Write the appropriate numbers (**i–x**) in boxes 13–18 on your answer sheet.*

Note: *There are more headings than sections so you will not use all of them.*

Example	*Answer*
Section 1	**vi**

13   Section 2

14   Section 3

15   Section 4

16   Section 5

17   Section 6

18   Section 7

List of headings

i	Class Handouts	**ii**	Final Assessment
iii	Homework	**iv**	Useful Information
v	Course Assessment	**vi**	Course Outline
vii	Study Resources	**viii**	Notification of Results
ix	College Facilities	**x**	Attendance

Portshead Community College

Dear Student,

Welcome to Portshead Community College. I hope you will enjoy your course here and that you will make some new friends as well as learn a lot.

1. _____

The syllabus which accompanies this letter gives you information about the topics that will be covered during your course.

2. _____

At each class you will receive study materials. You should keep them well organised in a file with dividers for each section and bring them with you to each class. Arrange for a 'study buddy' to collect materials for you if you are absent.

3. _____

Your teachers will often give you tasks to do outside of class time. These are an important part of the course and will contribute to your final grades. You will need to develop the ability to work independently and to organise your time.

4. _____

Passing your course will depend on 3 things:

    performance in class and on class activities and projects

    your results in the final test

    your attendance.

You will receive a short report halfway through each course which will include your teachers' assessments and test results. The final test takes place in the last week of the term.

5. _____

You will only be eligible to sit the end-of-course test if you attend 65 per cent or more of the lessons in that course. It is important that you attend regularly as low attendance will affect your results. Any student whose attendance falls below 65 per cent will not be eligible to sit the final test, which will automatically result in a fail.

6. _____

Those students who do not pass the course will receive a letter of attendance. Students who pass the course will receive a certificate of achievement.

7. _____

When you join this college you also become a member of the college library. In the library there are books, cassettes, videos and computer programs for you to use outside of class time.

I wish you success in your studies.

Molly Abbott

Program Manager.

Questions 19–25

The reading passage 'Student Accommodation' gives information about different types of accommodation available for students.

Using information from the reading passage, complete the sentences below **IN NO MORE THAN THREE WORDS**. *Write your answers in boxes 19–25 on your answer sheet.*

19 You cannot cook your own meals in full-board boarding houses or in

_____.

20 In a shared house, all the residents share the expenses of three things: rent,

_____.

21 The amount you pay to rent a house depends on

_____.

22 The accommodation that is available inside an academic institution is called

_____.

23 The purpose of a bond is to make sure that the tenant gives notice and doesn't

_____.

24 When you pay money to a landlord or agent, you should always get a

_____.

25 You should only sign an agreement after you are sure that you

_____.

STUDENT ACCOMMODATION

Although your accommodation is booked for the first few days, securing your long-term accommodation will be your own responsibility. During your orientation program, the housing options available will be discussed with you and you will be advised of the various organisations where you can go for help in finding accommodation.

You may find it more convenient to obtain accommodation in the institution where you are studying. Alternatively you may prefer to rent a room in a house or flat with other students. The various types of available accommodation are listed overleaf. The cost of accommodation will vary according to the facilities provided and the location.

The types of housing available include:

boarding houses

shared houses or flats

residential colleges

rented houses or flats.

Boarding houses: These are a combination of single and shared rooms which are rented out individually. There are two types of boarding houses available:

i) Self-cooking (you do your own cooking in a communal kitchen). Cooking and eating utensils are often provided.

ii) Full board (meals are cooked for you).

Facilities in a boarding house usually include: fully furnished room, linen, shared bathroom, gas/electricity charges.

Shared houses or flats: Shared accommodation is available when somebody has a spare room in their house or flat which they wish to rent. The rent and costs of gas/electricity are shared equally between the people sharing the flat. Each person is also expected to help clean and tidy the shared living space (e.g. kitchen, bathroom, living room). People sharing a house or flat are also responsible for cleaning their own room, doing their washing and cooking their own meals.

Residential colleges: Residential colleges are a feature of many academic institutions in Australia. The colleges are located on campus or very close to the campus and usually provide single study/bedrooms, shared bathroom, all meals and linen.

Rented houses or flats: These are usually for a longer term. Most flats are unfurnished and do not contain any furniture except a stove. Houses are considerably more expensive than flats, and rent varies with size, condition and location.

The costs of electricity and gas are additional. When renting a house or flat you can either sign a **lease** or enter into a **tenancy agreement** (written or verbal) with the landlord.

Landlords and managing agents usually require tenants to lodge an amount of money as a **bond**. A bond is kept by the landlord (or in some States by a Bond Board) as a protection against the tenant damaging the rented property or moving out without giving notice. If you have kept the place clean and not damaged it, you would be entitled to have the bond refunded when you leave.

Rules for Renting or Leasing

1) All agreements with landlords should be in writing. Make sure you fully understand any agreements **before you sign**.

2) Always inspect the place carefully **before** you move in and keep a list of any items that were damaged by previous tenants. This prevents problems when you claim the return of bond money.

3) For furnished flats, always compile a list of furniture and equipment. A copy should be held by you, and a copy held by the landlord or real estate agent.

4) Always get a **receipt** from the landlord/agent when you pay rent and keep these receipts and any agreement in a safe place. Make sure you have a receipt for any bond money you have paid.

5) Always give notice **in writing** at least one rental period before you intend moving out and retain a copy of the dated letter yourself.

SECTION 3   *Questions 26–40*

Questions 26–40 are based on the passage 'Foster Families in Rwanda'.

Questions 26–30

The passage has 17 paragraphs labelled A–Q.

Which paragraphs contain the following information?

*Write the appropriate letter **A–Q** in boxes 26–30 on your answer sheet. You only need **ONE** letter for each answer.*

Note: *You may use each letter more than once.*

Example	*Answer*
A schoolteacher who cares for orphans	**A**

26 The situation in orphanages.

27 The situation in refugee camps.

28 The number of children who have lost their families.

29 The kind of help which is given to foster families.

30 The story of a women trying to give her child to someone to look after.

Foster Families in Rwanda

A Sperantia Nyirantibenda vividly recalls the night she was unceremoniously turned into a foster parent by soldiers who brought her five children and two sacks of maize. They came knocking at her door in the town of Gitarama as the civil war in Rwanda was winding down. Nyirantibenda, a 34-year-old school teacher, nervously opened the door and immediately recognised the smiling faces before her. 'I have brought you children,' one of the soldiers told Nyirantibenda this time. 'I will see you later.'

B The maize the soldiers left behind did not last very long, and they never came back. Nyirantibenda is still caring for the children. She says she will gladly keep them so long as she receives some assistance.

C Food for the Hungry International (FHI), a US-based voluntary organisation supported by the UN High Commissioner for Refugees, has come in to help the school teacher. In Rwanda and Zaire, FHI supports families which have taken in orphans and lost children, as well as unaccompanied minors who have formed into groups to live together. Over 7000 people receive blankets, shelter materials and a regular supply of corn, beans and oil.

D FHI originally began the program to help children separated from their families at Mugunga camp, near Goma in eastern Zaire, one month after more than a million Rwandan refugees flooded into Goma in July 1994, fleeing victorious troops of the Rwandan Patriotic Front.

E An estimated 95 000 children were separated from their families during the war. Nearly half of them were inside Rwanda and the rest were in refugee camps in Zaire, Tanzania, Burundi and Uganda, which together hold more than 2.1 million refugees.

F At the outset of the refugee influx into Goma, conditions in the camps were appalling. Thousands of refugees were dying every day of cholera, dysentery and other diseases. Youngsters were being picked up beside bodies lying along the roads. Starving parents were abandoning their children or sending them to centres for unaccompanied minors in the camps.

G Rachel Poulton, an FHI spokesperson in Gitarama, said that during a visit to a tent for separated children, a 5-year-old girl followed her and asked for help. She said her parents were dead. The girl kept glancing over her shoulder at a woman who Poulton subsequently discovered was her mother. The woman later told Poulton she could no longer feed her daughter.

H Poulton said that, over a four-day period, 184 children arrived at the tent and 16 others were brought by elders. 'There were also a lot of people

fostering—mostly grandmothers and aunts. And there were sibling groups,' she said. She said that a system was developed whereby FHI supported groups of unaccompanied children.

I 'The challenge was to support these children in the community rather than in institutions. This shows another way of caring,' Poulton said. She said that it was preferable for children to grow up in a family setting rather than in orphanages.

J Myra Adamson, a 63-year-old nurse, born in South Africa to American missionary parents, works with care givers and foster parents living in bombed-out houses in Kigali. 'These separated children in the communities need food. They need someone to give them stability. They need someone they can turn to,' she said. 'The family would be destroyed if the children were brought to orphanages.'

K While a large proportion of children—about 60 per cent—are with foster families or ad hoc groups, a large number of unaccompanied minors also turn up in orphanages, such as the red-brick compound of Saint Andrew's church at Kabgayi. Run by Abundant Life International—an organisation of former Rwandan exiles from Uganda—this orphanage was started 3 months ago and it now houses 536 children. The youngsters were either brought to the institution or fetched by workers who had been informed of their location.

L 'Soldiers would come to us to tell us where we could find children and we would go and pick them up,' said an official. He said he himself had packed in his car 30 children he had picked up from nearby Kibuye prefecture where camps for displaced people had been closed. 'We get groups of 60, 70 children,' he said.

M Throughout Rwanda and Zaire, United Nations International Children's Fund (UNICEF) and several other relief organisations are not only supporting various programs for unaccompanied minors, but are also pooling resources to help track missing relatives. As of March, over 7000 children had been reunited with their families.

Questions 31–35

Complete the table below by writing **NO MORE THAN THREE WORDS** *in boxes 31–35 on your answer sheet.*

Location	Person or organisation	Activity
Gitarama	*Example* **Nyirantibenda**	looking after five children
....(31).....	FHI	started helping lost children
.....(32).....	Rachel Poulton	working for FHI
Rwanda and Zaire	.....(33).....	finding relatives and reuniting families
Kigali	.....(34).....	nursing
Kabgayi	Abundant Life International	.....(35).....

Questions 36–40

Do the statements below agree with the information given in the text?

In the boxes 36–40 on your answer sheet write:

TRUE   *if the statement is true*

FALSE   *if the statement is false*

NOT GIVEN   *if the information is not given in the passage*

36   FHI prefers to put orphaned children into orphanages.

37   Nyirantibenda's own children were killed during the war.

38   FHI also supports groups of children who are looking after themselves and not in the care of adults.

39   More than half of the orphans are being looked after in orphanages.

40   FHI first started helping unaccompanied Rwandan children in Zaire.

IELTS PRACTICE TEST

GENERAL TRAINING READING

TEST 2

TIME ALLOWED: 1 hour

NUMBER OF QUESTIONS: 40

Instructions

All answers must be written on the answer sheet

The test is divided as follows:

Section 1	*Questions 1–14*
Section 2	*Questions 15–27*
Section 3	*Questions 28–40*

Start at the beginning of the test and work through it. You should answer all questions.

If you cannot do a particular question, leave it and go on to the next. You can return to it later.

SECTION 1   Questions 1–12

Questions 1–7 apply to the reading passage 'National Cycle Network'.

ROADS FOR PEOPLE! HELP CREATE A
National Cycle Network

The figures speak for themselves. Over 20 million cars are registered in Britain and road traffic is projected to at least **double** by the year 2025.

Twice as much traffic on your roads... Imagine it !

Yet many more people would **choose** to make their shorter journeys by cycle—if only the road conditions felt safe.

Now, an answer to this problem is being created.

THE 5000-MILE NATIONAL CYCLE NETWORK

For fifteen years, Sustrans—it stands for 'sustainable transport'—has been building traffic-free routes for cyclists and walkers, often through the heart of towns and cities. Several hundred miles are now completed, using disused railway lines, canal towpaths, riversides and unused land. As a civil engineering charity, we work in partnership with local authorities and landowners.

We are now promoting a true national network, composed of traffic-free paths, quiet country roads, on-road cycle lanes and protected crossings.

Safe cycling networks already exist in many parts of Europe—including Denmark, Germany, Switzerland and the Netherlands. Europeans are often astonished at the road dangers we put up with here.

A Danish cyclist is *ten times* less likely to be killed or seriously injured—per mile cycled—than a cyclist in Britain. Extensive national and local cycle routes there are supported by slower traffic systems on surrounding roads.

A national cycle network for Britain can help transform local transport for the twenty-first century. With your help, it really is achievable! Make a donation now!

Questions 1 and 2

*Answer the questions by choosing the appropriate letters **A–D** and writing them in boxes 1–2 on your answer sheet.*

1   Sustrans is

    A   a local authority

    B   a construction company

    C   a civil engineering charity

    D   a cycle network

2   How many cars are expected to be on Britain's roads in 2025 ?

    A   one million

    B   more than 40 million

    C   exactly 40 million

    D   twice as much traffic

Questions 3–7

*Answer the questions using **NO MORE THAN THREE WORDS** from the text for each answer. Write your answers in boxes 3–7 on your answer sheet.*

3   How many miles of the network have already been completed?

4   At what are other European cyclists surprised that British cyclists accept?

5   In addition to cycle networks, what does Denmark have to protect cyclists?

6   How can people help create a national cycle network in Britain ?

7   Apart from cyclists, who benefits from the work of Sustrans?

Questions 8–14

Questions 8–14 apply to the reading passage 'Roads—the Facts' on the next page.

Do the following statements agree with the information given in the passage?

In the boxes 8–14 on your answer sheet write:

    TRUE   *if the statement is true*

    FALSE   *if the statement is false*

    NOT GIVEN   *if the information is not given in the passage*

8 There might be three times as many cars in rural areas in 2025.

9 The levels of air pollution in British cities are often higher than the standards set by the World Health Organization.

10 More German children go to school by car than British children.

11 It is believed that pollution from vehicles can make some children's illnesses worse.

12 Most of the national cycle network will be in country areas.

13 Most towns and cities will be only 10 minutes ride away from the national cycle network.

14 The national cycle network will cost the same as the national roads program.

ROADS—THE FACTS

In 1994 the Royal Commission on Environmental Pollution described 'the unrelenting growth of transport' as 'possibly the greatest environmental threat facing the UK'.

The Department of Transport predicts a doubling of traffic on 1988 levels by the year 2025. The Countryside Commission has warned that traffic through country areas may treble by then.

Vehicle exhaust is the major cause of urban air pollution. World Health Organization limits are regularly exceeded in most UK cities.

1 in 7 children suffers from asthma, thought to be exacerbated by traffic fumes.

Over 1500 wildlife sites including ancient woodlands and sites of special scientific interest are still threatened by road building.

Four times as many junior-age children are driven to school in Britain as in Germany, because of road dangers. In Holland 60 per cent of children cycle to school—compared with only 2 per cent here.

The National Cycle Network will

• Cater for all users—commuters, school-children, shoppers, family groups.

• Run right through the middle of most major towns and cities, enabling over 20 million people to ride to their nearest town centre within 10 minutes!

• Cost the equivalent of just a few weeks of the current national roads program.

• Be professionally designed and engineered, in cooperation with local authorities and landowners, to create high quality routes.

With your help we can build a network of commuter and leisure paths for a safer, healthier future.

SECTION 2   Questions 15–27

Questions 15–27

The text about St. Trinian's College on the following page gives the answers to questions commonly asked by the college's applicants.

There are seven sections A–G.

*Choose the most suitable question-heading for each section from the list below. Write the appropriate numbers (**i–x**) in the correct boxes on your answer sheet.*

Note: *There are more question-headings than sections so you will not use all of them.*

Example	Answer
Section A	**vi**

15   Section B
16   Section C
17   Section D
18   Section E
19   Section F
20   Section G

List of question-headings

i   Which course should I apply for?

ii   Are the courses full-time or part-time?

iii   Are there a lot of rules?

iv   How much does it cost?

v   What level of education do I need to enter the college?

vi   How can I apply?

vii   Can the college help me to get a job?

viii When do courses start?

ix   What assistance is given to foreign students?

St. Trinian's College

What applicants usually want to know—the questions we are most commonly asked.

A _____

You can either phone for an interview or complete the attached form indicating which course you would like to take and return it to us by post, enclosing the registration fee.

B _____

If you have difficulty in deciding which program would most effectively meet your needs, our academic counsellors can help you.

C _____

Our tuition fees are listed on the back of the enrolment form.

D _____

All long courses follow the academic year, but with short courses this is not possible. Full details of term dates will be mailed to you on request.

E _____

Our overseas student office will assist with immigration procedures and can also give advice on accommodation and other matters. We do everything we can to help overseas students settle in.

F _____

Most of our courses include curriculum vitae writing and interview skills. Through our extensive contacts in the local business community we are often in a position to help graduates find suitable employment.

G _____

The college is a friendly place and has a pleasant, relaxed atmosphere. The few regulations that are enforced are mainly a matter of common sense, concerned with respecting the rights of fellow students and staff. For students studying practical, job training courses, it is compulsory to wear clothing which is appropriate to their workplace.

Questions 21–27

The following form gives information on the terms and conditions of enrolment of a college.

Answer these questions in **NO MORE THAN THREE WORDS**.

Write your answers in boxes 21–27 on your answer sheet.

21   Who does the college inform if a student does not attend classes?

22   If a student cannot speak English well, what does he or she have to agree to do first?

23   Who provides pens, pencils, books and other equipment?

24   Course fees cannot be paid in cash. How do course fees have to be paid?

25   What happens to an application fee if the course is cancelled?

26   To obtain the maximum refund, what is the shortest notice of withdrawal a student can give?

27   If a student wants to change courses and go to a different college, to whom must he or she apply?

TERMS AND CONDITIONS OF ENROLMENTS

Full-fee paying international students are required to:

* study on a full-time basis

* comply with the visa regulation that at least 90 per cent attendance must be maintained. The college is required to notify the immigration authorities of unsatisfactory attendance which may result in the termination of the visa

* have adequate English language proficiency for the selected mainstream course or undertake to do an ELICOS course first

* have adequate financial means to do the course

* participate in orientation activities.

Note: You are advised to read and understand the conditions set out in the government acceptance advice form when you sign the declaration because you are required to comply with those conditions as an international student in Australia.

FEES

Application fees

The non-refundable application fee is $100.

Course fees

1. The course fees set for 1997/1998 are:

Certificate Courses	A$ 10 200	per year
Advanced Certificate Courses	A$ 10 200	per year
Associated Diploma Courses	A$ 10 200	per year
ELICOS	A$ 5 950	20 weeks
VCE	A$ 5 600	20 weeks

2. The annual course fee includes the full cost of tuition and educational services provided by the college. Textbooks, equipment, tools, stationery and any other individual requirements that you may need in your studies are your responsibility.

3. Fee payment instructions are notified in the letter of provisional acceptance and fees must be paid by the date specified in the letter.

4. All tuition fees must be paid by bankdraft and made payable to King George's College of TAFE.

REFUND POLICY

Application fees

a) The application fee will not be refunded if the application is withdrawn after an offer of place has been made.

b) Application fees will be refunded if the application is rejected or the course is cancelled by the college.

Course fees

If a student withdraws after payment of fees, the following will apply:

a) If notice of withdrawal is received by the college less than two (2) weeks before the course commences, no refund is given.

b) If written notice of withdrawal is given to the college less than four (4) weeks but more than two (2) weeks before the commencement of the course, 50 per cent of the course fee will be refunded.

c) If written notice of withdrawal is received by the college at least (4) weeks before the course commences, 80 per cent of the tuition fee will be refunded.

All notices of withdrawal must be in writing and addressed to the Manager, International Student Programs.

The notice of withdrawal should state name, course, date of commencement and reason for withdrawal.

TRANSFER TO ANOTHER INSTITUTION

Applications for transfer must be made in writing to International Student Programs stating reasons, and a copy of the acceptance letter from the receiving institution must be attached. Fees to be transferred will be subject to the refund policy.

Note: The college will not be responsible for any monies made payable to any agent.

SECTION 3 Questions 28–39

Questions 28–31

The passage 'The Panda's Last Chance' has 6 paragraphs labelled A–F.

Which paragraphs contain the following information?

*Write the appropriate letters **A–F** in boxes 28–31 on your answer sheet. You only need **ONE** letter for each answer.*

Note: *You may use each letter more than once.*

Example	Answer
Where panda habitats are located.	**A**

28 The separation of panda groups.

29 The panda's diet.

30 The illegal killing of pandas.

31 Why pandas' living areas have been reduced.

THE PANDA'S LAST CHANCE

Chinese authorities have devised an ambitious plan to save the giant panda from the ravages of deforestation. Martin Williams assesses the creature's chances of avoiding extinction.

A   The giant panda, the creature that has become a symbol of conservation, is facing extinction. The major reason is loss of habitat, which has continued despite the establishment, since 1963, of 14 panda reserves. Deforestation, mainly carried out by farmers clearing land to make way for fields as they move higher into the mountains, has drastically contracted the mammal's range. The panda has disappeared from much of central and eastern China, and is now restricted to the eastern flank of the Himalayas in Sichuan and Gansu provinces, and the Qinling Mountains in Shaanxi province. Fewer than 1400 of the animals are believed to remain in the wild.

B   Satellite imagery has shown the seriousness of the situation; almost half of the panda's habitat has been cut or degraded since 1975. Worse, the surviving panda population has also become fragmented; a combination of satellite imagery and ground surveys reveals panda 'islands' in patches of forest separated by cleared land. The population of these islands, ranging from fewer than ten to more than 50 pandas, has become isolated because the animals are loath to cross open areas. Just putting a road through panda habitat may be enough to split a population in two.

C The minuscule size of the panda populations worries conservationists. The smallest groups have too few animals to be viable, and will inevitably die out. The larger populations may be viable in the short term, but will be susceptible to genetic defects as a result of inbreeding.

D In these circumstances, a more traditional threat to pandas—the cycle of flowering and subsequent withering of the bamboo that is their staple food—can become literally species-threatening. The flowerings prompt pandas to move from one area to another, thus preventing inbreeding in otherwise sedentary populations. In panda islands, however, bamboo flowering could prove catastrophic because the pandas are unable to emigrate.

E The latest conservation management plan for the panda, prepared by China's Ministry of Forestry and the World Wide Fund for Nature, aims primarily to maintain panda habitats and to ensure that populations are linked wherever possible. The plan will change some existing reserve boundaries, establish 14 new reserves and protect or replant corridors of forest between panda islands. Other measures include better control of poaching, which remains a problem despite strict laws, as panda skins fetch high prices; reducing the degradation of habitats outside reserves; and reforestation.

F The plan is ambitious. Implementation will be expensive—Yuan 56.6 million (US$ 12.5 million) will be needed for the development of the panda reserves—and will require participation by individuals ranging from villagers to government officials.

Questions 32–33

There are several problems affecting the panda. From the list below, choose 2 more problems which are mentioned in the reading passage.

*Write the appropriate numbers (**i–vi**) in boxes 32 and 33 on your answer sheet.*

i	pandas prefer to inbreed
ii	panda groups are getting too small
Example	
iii	**panda habitats have shrunk**
iv	pandas move to other countries
v	more bamboo is withering
vi	panda groups are isolated

Questions 34–40

Below is a summary of the reading passage 'The Panda's Last Chance'. Complete the summary by choosing words from the box following the summary. Write your answers in boxes 34–40 on your answer sheet.

Note: *There are more words than spaces so you will not use them all. You may use any word more than once.*

The survival of the giant panda is being seriously threatened. Panda numbers have already seriously .....(34)..... . This is largely because the overall size of their habitat has been reduced and habitable areas are now .....(35)..... from each other. Two results are that pandas are more prone to genetic .....(36)..... and are unable to move around freely to follow the .....(37)..... cycles of the bamboo that they eat. A new plan is aiming to protect the existing panda habitats and to .....(38)..... many of them. This plan also includes reforestation and the creation of new .....(39)..... . To succeed, everyone, including both the government and individuals, will have to .....(40)..... .

survival	disconnected	dominated
decreased	problems	join
increased	growth	reserves
food	cooperate	disconnect

IELTS PRACTICE TEST

GENERAL TRAINING READING

TEST 3

TIME ALLOWED: 1 hour

NUMBER OF QUESTIONS: 40

Instructions

All answers must be written on the answer sheet

The test is divided as follows:

Section 1	*Questions 1–12*
Section 2	*Questions 13–25*
Section 3	*Questions 26–40*

Start at the beginning of the test and work through it. You should answer all questions.

If you cannot do a particular question, leave it and go on to the next. You can return to it later.

SECTION 1   Questions 1–12

Questions 1–2

Read the following advertisement and answer the questions. Choose the appropriate letters A–D and write them in boxes 1–2 on your answer sheet.

THE FUN WAY TO SAVE!

Join the **Woolwich for Kids Club** and you can save money and earn interest.

And you will have a lot of fun besides! As a club member, you will have your own passbook with a wallet to keep it in and your own special money box. Until you are thirteen we will send you the club magazine, edited by Henry's Cat, every six months. It is full of fun and games, news, quizzes, things to do and see, and great competitions to enter. When it is your birthday, Henry's Cat will send you a special birthday card.

If you are sixteen or under, **Woolwich for Kids Club** is specially for you. It's the fun way to save!

1   What is the Woolwich for Kids Club?

   A   a sports club

   B   a banking service

   C   a magazine

   D   a club for people who like cats

2 How many magazines do children receive each year?

A six

B twelve

C two

D one

Questions 3–6

MEDICARE

YOUR HEALTH INSURER

What does Medicare cover?

Doctors

Medicare helps pay for the doctor to treat you at the doctor's surgery or wherever you need treatment. Medicare helps pay for treatment by a specialist. If you need to see a specialist, you must be referred by your doctor.

Other medical services

- X-rays
- pathology tests
- medical tests, examinations and procedures

Optometrists

Medicare helps pay for eye tests, but not for the cost of glasses or contact lenses.

Dentists

Routine dental services are not covered. However, some medical-type operations performed by approved dentists are covered.

Hospitals

Public patient

If you choose to be treated under Medicare as a public patient in a public hospital, Medicare will cover all hospital costs. You pay nothing.

Private patient

If you choose to be treated as a private patient in any hospital, Medicare will help to pay for services by your doctor. However, Medicare will not pay for expenses such as theatre fees or your accommodation. These charges can be covered by arranging private health insurance.

Look at the following statements after reading the notice about Medicare.

In boxes 3–6 on your answer sheet write:

TRUE   if the statement is true

FALSE   if the statement is false

NOT GIVEN   if the information is not given in the notice

Example	Answer
Medicare does not pay for glasses.	**TRUE**

3 Medicare does not pay for any work done by dentists.

4 Medicare pays for ambulance fees.

5 If you have not seen a doctor first, Medicare will not pay for you to see a specialist.

6 Medicare will pay at least some hospital doctor's costs for both private and public patients.

Questions 7–12

You want to send some international mail.

Read the text 'International Postal Services' on the next page and answer questions 6–11 using **NO MORE THAN THREE WORDS** for each answer.

Write your answers in boxes 7–12 on your answer sheet.

7 If you do not pay enough postage for airmail, how may your letter or package be sent?

8 How much does it cost to send a postcard by airmail?

9 What does the post office use to follow the movement of priority mail?

10 Which is the best priority service if you want to send expensive jewellery abroad?

11 If you send something by either international recorded or international registered, what does the person receiving it have to do?

12 What kind of service is faster than swiftair?

INTERNATIONAL POSTAL SERVICES

GETTING THE PRICE RIGHT

It pays to get the postage right when you're sending mail abroad. Anything intended for airmail but underpaid stands the risk of being sent by surface mail instead. So make sure that you check the postage when mailing abroad.

STAMP BOOKS

For extra convenience, remember international stamp books. There are two available: 4 x 41p stamps with airmail labels, for sending 10 g letters anywhere outside of Europe. 4 x 35p stamps with airmail labels, for sending postcards to anywhere in the world.

PRIORITY TREATMENT

PRIORITY SERVICES FOR YOUR INTERNATIONAL MAIL

These three new services incorporate the latest barcode technology to track and trace your mail up to despatch from the United Kingdom.

1. INTERNATIONAL RECORDED

Peace of mind when posting abroad

Like using recorded delivery in Britain, this service gives you a signature on delivery and is recommended for items of little or no monetary value sent worldwide. Valuable items should be sent by the international registered service.

Priced at £2.50 per item plus airmail postage, it provides compensation to a maximum of £25.

Advice of delivery (documentary confirmation of delivery) is available for an extra 40p.

2. INTERNATIONAL REGISTERED

Greater security for your valuables

Gives you extra security in the UK and abroad, and a signature on delivery.

Available to 140 destinations, it costs £3.00 plus airmail postage for compensation up to £500; £4.00 plus airmail postage for compensation up to £1000.

Lower limits apply to some destinations; to others, registered is not available. Please check at your local post office. Advice of delivery (documentary confirmation of delivery) is available for an extra 40p.

3. SWIFTAIR

The express airmail service

Although it is not a courier service, and therefore cannot guarantee delivery the following day, swiftair is faster than ordinary airmail, international recorded and international registered. It is the economical alternative to courier services when next-day delivery is not essential.

Price £2.70 plus airmail postage.

SECTION 2   *Questions 13–25*

Questions 13–19

The following notice gives information about school excursions. Each excursion is labelled A–J.

SCHOOL EXCURSIONS

A   Ancient and Modern Museum

This is a museum with a difference. Along with the usual historical exhibits, this museum features an up-to-date display of hands-on information technology.

B   Shortlands Wildlife Park

This is not the usual 'animal gaol'. Here exotic animals wander free in large compounds, separated in such a way that they can't harm one another.

C   Botanical Gardens

Besides the many exotic plants one expects to see in a botanical garden, these gardens feature an array of native birds and other wildlife.

D   Wax World

If you're interested in seeing how people used to live and dress, Wax World is the place for you. Featuring over 100 wax models of famous people, this venue is well-suited to anyone interested in changing trends in clothing.

E   The Central Art Gallery

The art gallery has six chambers each exhibiting paintings from different periods, from the Middle Ages to the present. The walking tour, recorded on tape, is designed for visitors interested in art history and criticism.

F   Technology Park

In the planetarium you can observe features of the night sky, and learn about such historical events as the origin of the crab nebula. This excursion also includes a visit to the Satellite Mapping Centre.

G   Parliament

Students are met at the entrance by ushers who show them around the Houses. The tour includes the Hansard library, the grand lounge, government and opposition offices and the public gallery.

H   St. Cedric's Cathedral

With the Bishops' Throne as its central feature, this building is a classic example of the excesses of architecture. This excursion is a must for any student interested in sculpture and stained glass as art forms.

I   The Light Fantastic

Find out about the fascinating process of candle making. This factory also holds the additional attraction of illustrating the diverse uses that candles and other wax products can have—from the projection of film, to their use in the art of sculpture and decoration.

J   Trolland's Caves

These caves, situated below the hills to the north of the city, are entered via the Widmore River. The caves are home to colonies of glow worms that shine like stars on the ceilings and walls of the caves, casting an eerie light on the many stalagmites and stalactites.

*Answer questions 13–19 below by writing the appropriate letters **A–J** in boxes 13–19 on your answer sheet.*

Note: *You may use any letter more than once.*

Example	Answer
Which excursion would you choose if you are interested in famous people?	**D**

13 Which excursion would you choose if you wanted to know about the different uses of wax?

14 Where could students learn something about the animals of the country they are studying in?

15 On which excursion is it possible to learn something about the stars?

16 Which excursion would be suitable for students of fashion and design?

17 Which excursion would attract people interested in computers?

18 On which excursion would you expect to listen to an art critic?

19 On which excursion would you need to travel by boat?

Questions 20–25

The reading passage 'Vocational Training' comes from a book about studying in Australia.

Do the following statements correspond with the information given in the passage? In the boxes 20–25 on your answer sheet write:

TRUE   *if the statement is true*

FALSE   *if the statement is false*

NOT GIVEN   *if the information is not given in the passage*

20 There are more people studying in TAFE colleges than in any other kind of higher education institution.

21 TAFE qualifications are accepted anywhere in Australia.

22 Some TAFE colleges offer university degrees.

23 Each TAFE college specialises in teaching skills for working within one specific industry.

24 The next chapter deals with English language courses.

25 Certificates or diplomas from all private post-secondary institutions are recognised everywhere in Australia.

Chapter 5
VOCATIONAL TRAINING

Technical and Further Education

Australia's Technical and Further Education (TAFE) sector is a nationally recognised government system of vocational education and training and is the major provider of the skills required by the Australian workforce.

TAFE is the largest of the tertiary education sectors in Australia. It accounts for approximately 70 per cent of post-secondary education enrolments. There are 232 major TAFE colleges in Australia.

Although each state and territory administers its own system of TAFE, the qualifications they award are transferable throughout Australia. Although TAFE colleges cannot award tertiary-level degrees, some TAFE courses permit TAFE graduates to be admitted with advanced standing into degree courses offered by universities.

TAFE courses provide initial and further education at professional, para-professional, post-trade, trade and operative level. TAFE courses are developed in collaboration with industry and the community to ensure the most up-to-date education and training is provided.

Private Post-secondary Institutions

These private institutions are like TAFE colleges because they teach special skills for jobs but each one of them usually specialises in courses for one industry.

There are many private institutions in Australia offering a wide range of courses: English language (ELICOS, see Chapter 6), secretarial studies, data processing, pilot training, business and management, recreational courses and religious studies. (Other courses offered by private post-secondary institutions are listed in Chapter 7, Special Studies.)

If you successfully complete these courses you receive a qualification called a 'certificate' or 'diploma'. These are widely recognised by professional associations and industries in Australia, and are sometimes recognised by higher education institutions for credit. Before you undertake a course at a private post-secondary institution you should check that the certificate or diploma offered is appropriate for your particular purpose because some private institutions offer courses which are not recognised. If you want to enter a higher education institution from a private post-secondary institution, you should ask the higher education institution whether they accept the qualification before you start your course.

SECTION 3   *Questions 26–40*

Questions 26–40 are based on the reading passage below.

UNDERGROUND CITIES—JAPAN'S ANSWER TO OVERCROWDING

A nation running out of room seeks a down-to-earth solution

The Japanese may find a solution to the nation's space shortage right beneath their feet. Some of Japan's largest construction companies are planning underground cities that would not only ease urban crowding but also provide protection against earthquakes and increase energy efficiency.

Japan's soaring real-estate prices provide reason enough. In a country with nearly half as many people as the United States, but squeezed onto an archipelago which is only one hundredth the size, land shortages have led to construction becoming prohibitively expensive.

Another plus for subterranean construction is that the underground earth's movement during an earthquake is far less than the surface's—a big consideration in earthquake-prone Japan. The devastation caused by recent earthquakes in Japan could to some extent have been avoided if much of the cities affected were largely located underground.

In addition, the near-constant temperature would reduce the fuel costs for subterranean cities. Underground areas would need much less heating in winter and much less cooling in summer.

Taisei Corporation of Tokyo is planning a network of 'Alice Cities', named after the fictional Lewis Carroll heroine who fell down a rabbit hole into a wonderland. Taisei proposes turning cramped downtowns into airy underground spaces connected by subway trains and subterranean roads. The cities will be designed for self-sufficiency, but could be linked to sister cities by underground railway. Although some buildings and roads would remain above ground, much surface space would be freed up for trees and public parks.

Each Alice City would be divided into three sectors. The first sector, Town Space, would comprise verdant underground boulevards and open-air and atrium-type plazas—all free of automobile traffic. These boulevards and plazas will include shopping malls, entertainment complexes and fitness centres. Secondly, the Office Space sector will house business operations, hotels and parking lots. A solar dome above each office complex will ease feelings of claustrophobia. Express elevators or an extension of the underground railway system will run to the bottom level. Some workers will ride to work vertically from residential areas within the sector, while others will commute from the suburbs. Isolated from the town and office sectors will be the third sector, Infrastructure Space. This will contain facilities for power generation, regional heating and air-conditioning, waste recycling, and sewage treatment.

Existing cities could be redeveloped beneath the surface using the Alice system. The downtown areas could be retained above ground in a slightly modified form and most of the future growth of the cities could be accommodated underground.

An alternative to the Alice City concept is the Shimizu Corporation's proposed Urban Geo Grid, a vast network of smaller subterranean city spaces linked by tunnels. The $80.2 billion project would cover 485 square miles and accommodate a half-million people.

The Urban Geo Grid provides for a much more complicated interaction of many underground spaces over a larger area. Each 'grid station'—a complex of underground offices, shopping malls and hotels—would be connected to several smaller 'grid points', which would provide local services such as public baths and convenience stores. The Grid would provide a network for road and rail transportation, communication, and energy supply both within a city and between cities. Individual facilities for various services such as power generation and waste treatment will be on a smaller scale, but more numerous.

Whichever concept is ultimately applied, one obstacle that will need to be overcome before Japanese cities have *real* 'downtowns' involves the nation's geology. Japan's densely populated lowlands are mostly founded on loose geologic strata, making underground construction particularly difficult. Thus, Japanese construction firms are conducting extensive research and development on technologies for drilling, excavation and underground construction.

Some of the technology is already available. Robots similar to those that built the Channel Tunnel between France and England could be used for excavation and construction in some areas. It is anticipated that within 10 to 15 years most of the remaining technological obstacles will be overcome.

Underground city spaces in Japan are therefore coming much closer to reality. It may be difficult to imagine people adapting to life underground, but in Japan it may be one of the most practical solutions to the problem of limited living space. The next century may see many similar developments in other countries.

Questions 26–30

Indicate whether the following characteristics apply to Alice Cities or Urban Geo Grids or both or neither by writing:

AC	*if it applies to Alice Cities*
UGG	*if it applies to Urban Geo Grids*
BOTH	*if it applies to both*
NEITHER	*if it applies to neither Alice Cities nor Urban Geo Grids*

in boxes 26–30 on your answer sheet. The first one has been done as an example.

Example	Answer
named after a storybook character	*AC*

26 cities linked by underground railways

27 a large number of separate underground spaces linked together

28 one large space for city facilities such as waste treatment

29 cities largely independent

30 construction has already started

Questions 31–35

*Using information from the reading passage, complete the sentences below **IN NO MORE THAN THREE WORDS**.*

31 Real estate is expensive in Japan because_____.

32 By moving many buildings and roads underground, surface land in Alice Cities could be used for_____.

33 In Alice Cities, some people will live in the sector called_____.

34 Underground cities in Japan cannot yet be built because of two factors: loose geologic strata and_____.

35 In the Urban Geo Grid, hotels would be located in the _____.

Questions 36–40

The following is a brief summary of the reading passage. Complete each gap in the summary by choosing a word from the box below the summary. Write your answers in boxes 36–40 on your answer sheet.

Note: *There are more words than gaps so you will not need to use them all. You may use any word more than once.*

Summary

Example
Japan is planning underground cities to solve problems of living space, **earthquakes** and energy.

One Japanese company plans to develop large cities underneath existing .....(36)..... areas. Each of these cities would be divided into three sectors: for .....(37)..... , office and infrastructure spaces. Another company plans a more spread out and complicated .....(38)..... based on smaller spaces. The main .....(39)..... to the construction of these cities is the unstable structure of the .....(40)..... itself.

obstacle	network	ground	technology
robots	earthquakes	developing	leisure
downtown	private	rural	

General Training Writing

About the Writing Test

The IELTS General Training Writing test takes 60 minutes. You have to complete two writing tasks.

Task 1
- you have about 20 minutes
- you must write a **letter** of at least 150 words
- you are given a problem and you must write a letter explaining a situation and/or requesting information or action. You may also have to talk about your needs, wants, likes, dislikes and/or to give opinions.

Task 2
- you have about 40 minutes
- you must write an **essay** of at least 250 words
- your answer should be like an essay you would write for a teacher or course tutor
- you are given a problem or an argument/point of view. In your answer, you may have to:
  describe the situation in your own country
  give your opinion and explain why you have that opinion
  agree or disagree with a statement.

Tasks 1 and 2
For both Tasks the following points apply.
- The topics of the questions will be of general interest, and no specialist knowledge is required. For example, topics can include *travel, accommodation, current affairs, shops and services, health and welfare, health and safety, recreation, social and physical environment.*
- You must write in complete sentences. Notes are **not** acceptable.

- Do not copy whole sentences or long phrases from the question. The examiner will recognise them, and they will not count towards the minimum number of words you must write.
- You may write on the question sheet if, for example, you want to underline key words or to write notes. (The person who marks your writing will not see the question sheet.)

How Answers are Assessed

- Task 1 and Task 2 are marked separately, i.e. when the marker is assessing your answer to one task, he/she will not look at or consider your response to the other task.
- Task 2 is longer and therefore it is more important in calculating your final mark. For example, if you get Band 6 in Task 1 and a Band 5 in Task 2, your overall mark will be Band 5. However, **both questions must be answered satisfactorily** in order to get a good overall mark. If you write a very good answer to one task and do not attempt the other task, your overall score will be much lower.
- When assessing your writing, the examiner looks at three things:
    content (the information and ideas)
    organisation (how the information and ideas are organised)
    language (sentence structure, vocabulary, etc.)

You should not neglect any of these aspects. For example, if the grammar and vocabulary of your answer are good but the content and organisation are poor, your score will be lower.

Writing Strategies

To answer Task 1 and Task 2 questions, you should work through the following steps.

> Step 1   Analyse the question
> Step 2   Make notes of ideas which could be useful
> Step 3   Make a plan
> Step 4   Write the letter or essay
> Step 5   Check for mistakes

In this section the five-step strategy will be used to guide you through various sample writing tasks for both Task 1 and Task 2.

Task 1

When the IELTS marker looks at a Task 1 answer, he or she has three basic questions in mind:
- Does the letter do what the question asks? Or, is the content (the ideas and information) appropriate to the task?

- Is the letter written in a well-organised, logical way?
- Is the language accurate and correct?

Many candidates get lower band scores in the test because the content and organisation of their writing are not good enough. It is important that you follow these steps when answering a Task 1 question.

Demonstration—Question

Sample Question 1

The course director of your previous college has invited you to attend a party for new students, and he has also asked you to give a talk about studying overseas. You have an important examination on the same day so you cannot attend the party.

Write to the director to apologise and to explain why you cannot attend. Suggest another date when you could give your talk.

How to Answer

STEP 1—ANALYSE THE QUESTION

What is the topic?
Find out by underlining the key words in the question.

The course director of your previous college has <u>invited</u> you to <u>attend a party</u> for new students, and he has also asked you to <u>give a talk</u> about studying overseas. You have an important examination on the following day so you <u>cannot attend the party</u>.

You have been invited to go to a party and give a talk, but you cannot go to the party.

To whom am I writing?
The letter is to the course director of your old college. Although you know him it is unlikely that you know him very well. The style of the letter should in this instance be **formal** or **semi-formal**.

What is your purpose in writing the letter?

Write to the director to <u>apologise</u> and to <u>explain why you cannot attend</u>. <u>Suggest another date</u> when you could give your talk or some other solution.

You can see that you are given **three** things to do:
- apologise (for not being able to attend)
- explain (why you cannot attend)
- suggest (another date).

STEP 2—MAKE NOTES OF IDEAS

Make a brief note of any ideas which you might use in your answer.
In the following box, the student has written some notes. On the right side is an explanation of what these notes mean.

thanks	thank the director for the invitation
saw friends	say that you saw some college friends last week
imp. exam	explain why the exam is important
date fixed	explain why the date of the exam cannot be changed
new coll.	talk about your new college
family well	talk about your family
all well there?	ask how everyone is at the old college
party details?	ask for details of the party
hope success	say that you hope the party is a success
sorry	say you can't come to the party and apologise
will talk about...	explain what you will say in your talk about studying overseas
first time	explain it is the first time you have ever been asked to give a talk like this
can come...	say when you can come
my tel.	tell the director how to contact you

STEP 3—MAKE A PLAN

Decide which of these ideas you will definitely use in the letter. Organise them. The notes from step 2 are on the left side below. In the box on the right there is a sample plan which is based on the notes. Each black dot represents a separate paragraph. Notice that not all of the ideas have been used.

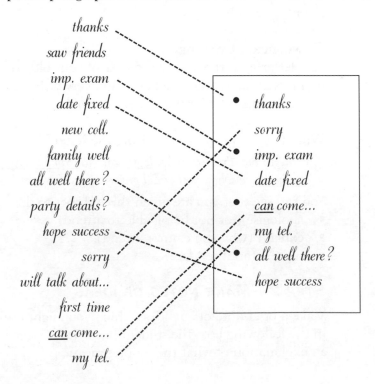

Follow the plan.

Demonstration—Letter

Dear Mr Arnold,

Thank you for ~~you~~ *your* kind invitation ~~for~~ *to* attend the party for new student*s* on the 29th of January. Thank you also for thinking of me to give a talk. However, unfortunately I am unable to attend the party.

I *am* afraid that on the following day I have my first semester ~~ekonomi~~ *economics* exam. This is ~~the~~ *a* complicated subject and a good ~~note~~ *mark* is essential for me, so I ~~must~~ have to spend the day before ~~to~~ studying. I ~~ask~~ *asked* my lecturer if it ~~will~~ *would* be possible to take the examination on another date, but this is not ~~permitting~~ *permitted*.

However, I would be very happy to give the talk on another date. I am available on the 5th and 6th of ~~febuary~~ *February*. If one of those date*s* ~~are~~ *is* convenient for you, please ~~to~~ let me know. I can be contacted ~~in~~ *at* the address above or ~~for me~~ *by fax* or telephone.

I hope that everyone at the college is well, and I hope that your party ~~will be~~ *is a great* success. I look forward to hearing from you.

Yours sincerely,

Aung San Nilar

Analysis and Practice

STEP 1—ANALYSE THE QUESTION

When analysing the question, you want to know:
- What is the situation or topic?
- Who is the addressee? In other words, to whom is the letter addressed? (This determines how formal the letter should be.)

- What is the purpose of writing the letter? (e.g. to request, to complain, to suggest?)

Task 1 questions are usually in two parts. The first part describes the situation or topic. The second part tells you to whom your letter should be addressed and gives you a task (or purpose).

The best way to identify these pieces of information is to <u>underline</u> the key words as you read carefully through the question. (Remember you are allowed to write on the question sheet.) Look again at the sample underlining in Step 1 in the Demonstration answer.

ACTIVITY 24

Read Sample questions 2 and 3 carefully and underline the key words. Then complete the tables under each question.

Sample Question 2

You have just spent a weekend staying at the Lilo Hotel in Adelaide. When you get home you find that you have left a bag at the hotel.

Write to the manager of the hotel and enquire whether the bag has been found. Give any relevant information about the bag and its contents. Ask the manager to contact you immediately if the bag is found and tell him/her how the bag can be sent to you.

Topic/Situation	*bag left at the hotel*
Addressee	*the hotel manager*
Purpose	*ing to enquire about your bag left ...*

Sample Question 3

You and some friends had dinner in a restaurant a few nights ago. The service at the restaurant was terrible and the food was bad. You and two friends had severe stomach-aches the following day. The food was also overpriced.

Write to the manager of the restaurant and explain these problems. Give any details that you think are relevant. Ask the manager to do something about the situation.

Topic/Situation	Terrible service, bad food & overpriced
Addressee	To the manager the restaurant
Purpose	To improve the quality of service, food and decrease the price

Check your answers in the Answer Key.

STEP 2—MAKE A NOTE OF IDEAS

Here you should make a brief note of *any* ideas which come to mind and which *may* be relevant. At this stage you do not have to decide exactly which ideas will be used in your writing. (Selecting which ideas to use is done in Step 3.)

The purpose of Step 2 is to help you think of information which is useful for the writing task. The process of quickly noting any ideas which come to mind will help you to access relevant information in your memory.

Remember also that these notes are for you only—the assessor will not see them—so the notes should be as brief as possible.

ACTIVITY 25

Quickly make notes of your ideas for both Sample questions in the previous activity.

Time target: 2 minutes for each question

STEP 3—MAKE A PLAN

At this stage you must think about two questions.
- Which ideas will definitely be used in the letter?
- How will these ideas be organised?

The letter should be divided into paragraphs. When you are planning the letter you should try to put your ideas into logical groups. Each of these groups will then become one paragraph.

There are several common patterns of letter organisation. You should learn these patterns so that your writing will then be organised in an English style. Firstly, all letters should have an **introductory paragraph** and a **closing paragraph**.

The introductory paragraph
In the introductory paragraph, there are several things you can do.

SAMPLE SENTENCES

	Formal	Less formal
greet the addressee (if he/she is your friend)		• Dear Jack, Hi. How are you? • Dear Annie, Hello. I hope everything is fine.
tell the addressee who you are (if he/she does not know you)	• Dear Sir, I was a guest at your hotel from 23 to 25 May. • Dear Mr. Parker, I am a student at your college, enrolled in the cookery course.	
thank the addressee (if he/she has sent you a letter or done something else for you)	• Dear Mr. Lopez, Thank your for your invitation to the reunion party on 15 January. • Dear Mr. Hendrix, Thank you for your letter asking me about studying in Australia.	• Dear Peter, Thanks for the invitation. • Dear Alan, Thanks for your letter. It was nice to hear from you.
explain your reason for writing	• I am writing to advise you of the loss of my credit card. • I'd like to inquire about course details. • I am writing to complain about the poor service at your restaurant.	• I must tell you about a new movie I saw last week. • Can you help me? • I am very sorry I forgot to send you a birthday card.

The closing paragraph

The content of the closing paragraph depends on what you have written in the rest of your letter, but some possibilities are listed in the following table.

	SAMPLE SENTENCES	
	Formal	Less formal
If your letter is *making a request*:		
mention what the addressee will do	• Thank you for your attention to this matter.	• Thanks for your help.
	• I look forward to your prompt response.	• Please write soon.
If your letter is *giving an apology*:		
make a final apology	• Once again, I am sorry for any inconvenience caused.	• I hope I didn't cause you too much trouble.
	• Please accept my apologies once more.	• Sorry again!
If your letter is *making a complaint*:		
mention what the addressee will do	• I expect to hear from you very soon.	
	• Please give this matter your immediate attention.	
If your letter is *giving information*:		
• say you hope you have been helpful	• I hope this information will help you.	• I hope all this helps.
• offer more information	• Please feel free to contact me for more information.	• If I can tell you anything else, please call me.
If your letter is *making suggestions*:		
• say you hope you have been helpful	• I trust these suggestions have been useful.	• I hope these suggestions help.
• offer more help	• Please let me know if I can help any further.	• If there is anything else I can do, please call.

The 'body' of the letter

The body is the middle part of the letter which contains most of the important information. There are several standard patterns for organising the body of your letter in an English style. Look at the following examples.

Type of letter	Plan
If your letter is *making a request*	• introductory paragraph • explain the situation • details of your request • closing paragraph
If your letter is *giving an apology*	• introductory paragraph • explain why you must apologise • alternative plan (if appropriate) • closing paragraph
If your letter is *making a complaint*	• introductory paragraph • explanation problems • say what you think the addressee should do • closing paragraph
If your letter is *giving information*	• introductory paragraph • information • offer more information (if appropriate) • closing paragraph
If your letter is *making suggestions*	• introductory paragraph • make first suggestion • provide an alternative to this suggestion or make a second suggestion • closing paragraph

Note that the above plans are examples only. Sometimes, the test question(s) will give you more than one purpose for writing the letter. If this happens you will have to choose from two or more of the above plans. For example, the Demonstration letter on page 107 combines apologising and suggesting.

ACTIVITY 26

The following is an example of notes of ideas for Sample question 2 on page 108. The notes are in the box on the left and their meaning is explained on the right. The notes are followed by three plans.

Which is the best plan based on the notes? What is wrong with the other two?

not valuable	explain that the bag and contents are not valuable in dollars, but are important to you
bag lost	say that the bag is missing
found?	ask whether the bag has been found
send	ask the manager to send the bag
when at hotel	say when you stayed at the hotel
room no.	say which room you stayed in
enjoy hol.	say that you enjoyed your holiday
bag size	give the bag's size and colour
contents	describe the bag's contents
stolen?	explain that you think the bag may have been stolen
police?	ask if you should tell the police
reward	tell the manager you will offer a reward
contact me	ask the manager to contact you
thanks	thank the manager for helping you

Plan 1
- *bag lost*
  stolen?
  call police?
  reward
- *contact me*
  send
  not valuable
- *enjoy hol.*
  room no.
  when at hotel
- *thanks*

Plan 2
when at hotel
room no.
contact me
thanks
bag lost
contents
send
bag size
found?
not valuable

Plan 3
- *when at hotel*
  room no.
  bag lost
  found?
- *bag size*
  contents
  not valuable
- *contact me*
  send
- *thanks*

Check your answer with the Answer Key.

ACTIVITY 27

Based on your notes from Activity 25, write a plan for a letter to answer Sample question 3. Remember to keep the plan as brief as possible.

Time target: 1 to 2 minutes

Note: Do not check the Answer Key yet. Wait until you have finished Activity 28.

ACTIVITY 28

It is important that you include in your letter all the things that the task tells you to do. Look for key words like *write, explain, ask, give, tell*. Following are two sample plans for Sample question 3. Both of them omit some important information that is specifically required by the task. Read each plan and say what is missing in each case.

Plan 1

- *when had dinner*
    - *want to complain*
- *service bad*
    - *no menu*
    - *long wait for food*
    - *long wait for bill*
- *food bad*
    - *too salty*
    - *not fresh*
    - *stomach-ache*
- *expensive*
- *won't come again*

Plan 2

- *when had dinner*
    - *want to complain*
- *food bad*
    - *over-cooked*
    - *too spicy*
    - *small quantity*
    - *expensive*
- *my demands*
    - *free meal*
    - *free drinks*

Now re-check the plan you did in the previous activity. Does it omit anything? Compare your plan with the sample plan for Activity 27 in the Answer Key.

STEP 4—WRITE THE LETTER

When you write a letter using your plan, you should think about how to expand the points you have noted. For example, in the Demonstration letter the writer is supposed to *explain why he/she cannot attend the party*. Instead of just saying that he/she has a test, the letter says *what kind of test, why it is important*, and *how the writer tried—unsuccessfully—to reschedule it*. The task also instructs the writer to *suggest another date or some other solution*. In the letter, the writer *gave a choice of dates* and *gave several ways to be contacted*.

You should give information that is relevant and realistic. Remember also that you cannot give too much information about any one point because you have to finish **all** the main points of the question.

For the **beginning** and the **ending** of your letter, there are a limited number of options:

	Beginning	Ending
If you don't know the name of the addressee	• Dear Sir, • Dear Madam, • Dear Sir/Madam,	Yours faithfully,
If you know the surname of the person but he/she is *not* a close friend	• Dear Mr Jenkins, • Dear Ms Lang, • Dear Dr Spock,	Yours sincerely,
If the person is a friend	• Dear Sue, • Dear Michael,	• Best regards, • Best wishes, • Love,

Appropriate Language

In English, there are certain standard words and phrases that can be used when you want to make a request, suggestion, complaint, and so on. These are called *functions*. You should learn some of the common functions. Some examples are featured in the table below.

	Formal	Less formal
Apology	• I'm terribly sorry, but… • I am afraid I… • I must apologise about (not) _____ing…	• I'm very sorry but… • I am sorry about (not) _____ing…
Complaint	• I must complain about… • I am not satisfied with… • I feel something should be done about…	(no informal forms)
Request	• Could you please… • Could you possibly… • Would it be possible to… • I would be grateful if you would… • Would you mind _____ing… • I wonder if you could…	• Could you… • Can you… • I'd like you to… • Would you mind _____ing…
Making suggestions	• I'd like to suggest that… • May I suggest that… • Perhaps we could… • Could you please…	• How about… • What about… • Why don't we… • Let's…

Many English textbooks will teach you functions suitable for different situations. You should look at the books you have available (a list of recommended books is on page 156) and learn a wide range of functions for use in Task 1.

Be sure to note whether a function is used in formal or in less formal situations. For most Task 1 questions you will use formal language, but you may be asked to write informally, for example to a close friend.

Making changes and alterations while you write

Most students write in pencil when completing the test and make changes by using an eraser. However, this wastes time. The quickest way to make changes is to cross out (draw a line through) the unwanted words and write the new words after or above. The marker will ignore any words that are crossed out.

ACTIVITY 29

For Sample question 2, write a complete letter using the best plan from Activity 26.

Time target: 15 minutes

STEP 5—CHECK FOR MISTAKES

Under the pressure of writing in exam conditions, most students make errors they would not usually make. These errors are often very basic, and they do not give the marker a good impression of your knowledge of English. Consequently, it is very important that you save a few minutes at the end of the test time period to check your writing and correct any mistakes you find.

The check-list in the next activity includes the most common grammatical errors made by candidates. You should use this reference to check your own work. These corrections could make a difference to your final score.

ACTIVITY 30

Correct the grammatical errors in the samples below by crossing out the mistake and writing in the correct form.

a) **Subject/Verb agreement**

   If one of those dates are convenient, please let me know.
   They doesn't gets enough exercise.

b) **Plurals**

   A party for all new student will be held on Monday.
   Both childrens and adults are affected.
   There are many new problems for individuals.

c) **Subject/Verb/Object**

   I afraid that I have lost your invitation.
   There are various negative effects on families or society.

d) Tenses

Many of the TV programs in my country are coming from overseas.

Yesterday, I ask my lecturer about the test results.

Individuals can be negatively affect by television.

e) Modals

Therefore, I must have to spend the day studying.

Watching too much TV can to make people lazy.

Governments should exercising more control.

f) Word form

I hope that your party will be success.

The cat died, causing great unhappy.

g) Possessives

Thank you for you kind invitation.

My supervisor party was great.

h) Spelling, capitalisation and punctuation

The ceremony is on the 5th and 6th of february.

I am dreading my first semester ekonomi exam.

I like listening to peoples problems.

i) Articles

This is the complicated subject.

He comes from another part of country.

Check your answers with the Answer Key.

If you found it difficult to make these corrections, you probably need to study some more English grammar. In addition to the categories of mistakes mentioned in the check-list, you should also make sure that you can use the following grammar points correctly:

- pronouns
- connecting words (conjunctions)
- conditional sentences
- relative clauses
- prepositions

ACTIVITY 31

Below is a sample letter for Sample question 2. The letter has some mistakes in functions and grammar. Find the mistakes, cross them out and write the corrections.

Dear Mr Simpson,

I stay in your hotel on the 23rd and the 24th of october. I was stay in room 603. When I have arrived home I discovered I had left one of my bag at hotel. Could you please checking your Lost and Found department and see if my bag is there?

The bag is the small black leather document case with the narrow strap. Inside the bag you can find several business card, Mont Blanc fountain pen, small adress book and three copies of business proposal. Also a silver pocket calculator. These things is not very value in money terms, but they have a lot of personal value to me.

I would appreciate it if you could contact me as soon as possible, since I particularly need the proposals for a presentation this week. If you could send the bag to me by courier service I am most grateful. I have arranged payment for the service on delivery here.

Thank you for you help.

Yours sincerely,

Fatima Ferrangites

Check your answers with the letter in the Answer Key.

ACTIVITY 32

Read through and check the letter you wrote for Activity 29. Make corrections by crossing out the old words and writing the new ones above or after.

Time target: 2 minutes

ACTIVITY 33

Using your own plan for Sample question 3 (from Activity 27), write a complete letter. Then check what you have written and make changes as necessary.

Time target: 20 minutes

Compare your letter with the sample letter in the Answer Key.

Assessing your written work

The best way to assess your written work is to ask someone with a higher level of English than yours to read it. Remember that grammar is not the only criterion. The content and organisation of your letter are also very important, so make sure that whoever comments on your writing also considers these two aspects.

You can learn more about these things from books about writing in English. You should also use the guide *Assessing Your Own Writing* at the end of Writing Task 2.

Task 2

For Task 2 you must write a short essay, similar to the kind of task you might have to do for a teacher as part of a class assignment. The minimum number of words is 250.

As with Task 1, when the IELTS marker reads your essay, he or she will have three main questions in mind.

- Does the essay do what the question asks? (Is the content relevant?)
- Is the essay written in a well-organised, logical way?
- Is the language accurate and correct?

Many students concentrate on the third point, language, and neglect content and organisation. To make sure that the content and organisation of your essay are satisfactory, you must spend a few minutes thinking about and planning your essay **before you start to write**. You will also be able to write your essay more quickly because you already know **what** you want to write about.

The strategy for Task 2 is the same as for Task 1.

> Step 1   Analyse the question
>
> Step 2   Make notes of ideas
>   that might be included in the essay
>
> Step 3   Make a plan
>   by selecting the best ideas and organising them
>
> Step 4   Write the essay
>
> Step 5   Check for mistakes
>   and correct them

Demonstration—Question

Sample Question 4

Television is now widespread in all communities. Almost everyone has access to this medium on a daily basis. However, the effects of television are not always positive.

What are some of the negative effects of television? What can be done to minimise these bad effects?

Give reasons for your answer.

STEP 1—ANALYSE THE QUESTION

What is my audience?
Task 2 questions are usually said to be 'as part of a class assignment'. You should write the essay as though it was for a teacher.

What is the topic?
The key words in the first part of the question have been underlined below:

> _Television is now widespread in all communities. Almost everyone has access to this medium on a daily basis. However, the effects of television are not always positive._

The subject of the first two sentences is the general topic of _television_. This topic is limited or narrowed in the third sentence which specifies the 'effects' of television, in particular the _negative_ effects ('are not always positive' means _are sometimes negative_).

What is your purpose/task in writing?
The key words of the rest of the question are underlined below:

> _What are some of the negative effects of television? What can be done to minimise these bad effects?_
> _Give reasons for your answer._

Note that there are actually two questions or tasks in the one activity:

- to give some of the possible negative effects of television
- to explain how to prevent or limit these negative effects

STEP 2—MAKE NOTES OF IDEAS

The following is an example of the kind of notes you might write at this stage. The sample notes are written in the box. To the right is a brief explanation of what these notes mean.

The possible negative effects of television

expens.	expensive for the community
destr. cust.	destroys local customs
waste time	people (especially children) waste time
ads bad	bad influence of advertising
lazy	people become lazy
fam. life	destroys family life
pol.	can be used for bad political purposes
eyes	bad for the eyes
Am. cult.	spreads Western (especially American) culture including undesirable images: greed, violence, sex

How to minimise these effects

contr. TV	control TV content
contr. ads	control advertising
explain	explain effects to people
alt. entert.	encourage alternative entertainment
hours	limit broadcasting hours

Step 3—Make a Plan

Decide which of the ideas will definitely be used in your essay. Organise these ideas logically.

In the box below right is a sample plan written on the basis of these notes. Not all of the ideas have been used in the plan. Related points are grouped together into paragraphs (marked with black dots).

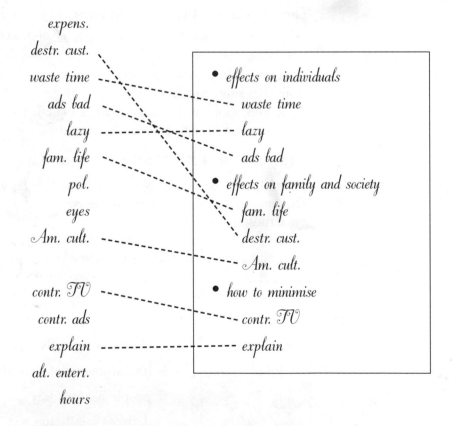

Step 4—Write the essay

Follow the plan.

Step 5—Check for mistakes

With ~~the~~ modern telecommunication**s** even people ~~which~~ *who* live in very remote areas have access to television. However, even though television is clearly very popular, ~~but~~ the effects *on* ~~to~~ people *of* watching television are often negative~~ly~~.

Individuals can be negatively affect*ed* in three main ways. Many people, both children**s** and adults, waste a lot of time sitting in front of a TV watching poor quality programs. Secondly, watching too much TV can ~~to~~ make people lazy and unhealthy because they ~~doesn't~~ *don't* get~~s~~ enough exercise. Thirdly, the advertisements on television can make people feel~~ing~~ unhappy with the thing**s** they *have* ~~has~~ and can influence them to spend money on new things.

TV has various ~~Various~~ negative effects on families and society. Because of TVs, families communicate less with each other and do less family activities together. Small societies may begin to lose their local customs if most television programs ~~will~~ come from another part of *the* country. Many of the TV programs in my *country come* ~~country are coming~~ from overseas, especially the United States of America,. *This* ~~and this~~ will affect national culture by encouraging the spread of western customs and values.

There ~~Although there~~ are two key ways to *minimise* ~~minimize~~ the negative effects described above. Firstly, governments should *exercise* ~~exercising~~ more control *over* ~~with~~ the content of TV programs. Programs which ~~they~~ are not educational or ~~which~~ may influence people in a negative way should be limited or restricted. Secondly, governments should *educate* ~~educating~~ people about the possible negative effects of TV. People can then regulate themselves and their children.

In conclusion, I think that ~~someone~~ *something* should ~~do~~ *be done* as soon as possible to protect the community from the negative effects of television. If the situation *is left* ~~will leave~~ to continue as it is, many new problem**s** for individual**s** and society will ~~be~~ arise in *the* future.

Analysis and Practice

STEP 1—ANALYSE THE QUESTION

The questions for Task 2 usually have two parts, a **topic paragraph** and a **question paragraph**.

Look again at Sample question 1:

> *Television is now widespread in all communities. Almost everyone has access to this medium on a daily basis. However, the effects of television are not always positive.*

introductory paragraph—gives you information or comment, helps to define the topic.

> *What are some of the negative effects of television? What can be done to minimise these bad effects?*

question paragraph—contains one, two or three questions. Tells you what information you must give about the topic.

> *Give reasons for your answer.*

You must read the question(s) carefully and do exactly what the task asks you to do. In order to answer the above Task successfully, this means:

1. Describe the possible negative effects of television.
2. Explain how these negative effects can be avoided or minimised.

In this task it is **not relevant** to, for example:
- discuss at length the *benefits* of television
- focus on other public media, for example radio or newspapers
- talk *only* about the effects of television *on children*
- discuss in great detail the fact that nearly everyone has access to television.

ACTIVITY 34

Sample questions 5 and 6 each have an **introductory paragraph** and a **question paragraph**. Read each Sample carefully and underline the key words. What do you have to talk about in your essays to answer the questions in a relevant way?

Sample Question 5

> *Many newspapers and magazines feature stories about the private lives of famous people. We know what they eat, where they buy their clothes and who they love. We also often see pictures of them in private situations.*

> *Is it appropriate for a magazine or newspaper to give this kind of private information about people?*

> *Give reasons for your answer.*

Sample Question 6

> *Many young people choose to continue their education at colleges or universities in English-speaking countries such as Britain, Australia or America.*
>
> *What are the benefits of studying abroad? What are some of the problems that students might experience when studying in a foreign country?*
>
> *Give reasons for your answer.*

Check your answers with the Answer Key.

STEP 2—MAKE NOTES OF IDEAS

As for Task 1, at this stage you should make brief notes of any ideas which come to mind and may be relevant. Later, in Step 3, choose the best ideas for your essay.

Candidates often have trouble thinking of ideas to include in their essay and waste a lot of time while they are writing trying to come up with more. If, before you start writing, you take two minutes to note anything which comes to mind, you will remember useful information and will also save time while you are writing.

Remember that these notes are only for your benefit. The assessor will not see them. The notes should be **as brief as possible**.

Giving your opinions

It will often be relevant to give your opinions in your essay. If the question can be answered with 'yes' or 'no', do not be afraid to **give a direct answer** (usually in the introduction or the conclusion of your essay).

Giving evidence or examples

You should use relevant evidence and/or examples to support any points that you make in your essay. This is very important. Your essay will be graded on the ideas you present and the way you support them. To understand how to do this, you should study the way that the sample Task 2 essays in this book support any points made.

ACTIVITY 35

You have already analysed Sample question 5 and Sample question 6 by underlining the key words. Now, quickly note any ideas which may be useful in you answer to these questions. Note that the **question paragraph** may have more than two questions in it.

Time target: 2 minutes for each question

STEP 3—MAKE A PLAN

Decide which of the ideas you have noted above will definitely be used in the essay. Organise these ideas into logical groups.

Your essay should be divided into **paragraphs**. In an essay of 250 words there should be between 4 to 7 paragraphs.

In the normal style of writing in English, each paragraph is usually limited to one aspect of the topic you are writing about. When you are planning your essay you should try to put the information that you want to use into logical groups. Each of these groups will then become one paragraph. (Look again at the Demonstration essay on page 123 for an example.)

If there are two or more questions in the **question paragraph** of a task, you should have at least one paragraph addressing each question in your essay. The following are examples of the format to be used when answering such an essay question.

	Plan 1	Plan 2
short paragraph	introduction	introduction
paragraph	answer to question 1	answer to question 1
paragraph	answer to question 2	answer to question 1 (continued)
paragraph	answer to question 3	answer to question 2
short paragraph	conclusion	conclusion

The pattern of organisation above in the right-hand column is used in the Demonstration essay.

Where you have two paragraphs answering one question, try to divide your ideas into two logical groups, one for each paragraph. In the Demonstration essay although there are two paragraphs talking about the first question ('What are some of the negative effects of television?'), the first of these paragraphs was about *effects on individuals* and the second was about *effects on families and societies*.

If there is only one question in the task (for example whether you *agree* or *disagree* with a statement given in the introductory paragraph), you could use the following patterns of organisation.

To agree	To disagree
short introduction	short introduction
reasons why the statement is incorrect	reasons why the statement is correct
reasons why the statement is correct	reasons why the statement is incorrect
more reasons why the statement is correct	more reasons why the statement is incorrect
short conclusion	short conclusion

In these examples, **both sides** of a situation or argument are discussed. It is a good idea to talk about both sides because this will give you more things to write about. However, if you do this, in the conclusion of your essay you should say which side, in your opinion, is stronger.

Alternatively you could analyse only one side of an issue. If you decide to discuss only one side, it is a good idea to state clearly in your introduction that it is the best point of view in your opinion.

To agree	To disagree
short introduction	short introduction
reason 1 supporting the statement	reason 1 opposing the statement
reason 2 supporting the statement	reason 2 opposing the statement
reason 3 supporting the statement	reason 3 opposing the statement
short conclusion	short conclusion

ACTIVITY 36

Using the ideas you noted in the previous activity, make a brief plan for each of Sample questions 5 and 6. Remember that the plan is only for you—the marker will not look at it—so be as brief as possible.

Note: Most essays written by native speakers of English have an introduction and a conclusion. However, for your essay the introduction and the conclusion should be very short and you do not actually need to mention them in your plan. They are mentioned in the patterns of organisation above just to remind you of the overall structure of the essay. (We will discuss what to write in introductions and conclusions in Step 4.)

Time target: 2 minutes for each plan

Compare your plans with the sample plans in the Answer Key.

STEP 4—WRITE THE ESSAY

The introduction
You should try to write a short (one or two sentences) introduction for your essay. The main purpose of an introduction is to tell the reader what you are going to write about. Your introduction must state the main issue (or the main focus) of the essay. Look at the first paragraph of the Demonstration essay again:

*With modern telecommunications, even people who live in very remote areas have access to television. However, **even though television is clearly very popular, the effects on people of watching television are often negative**.*

Notice that the second sentence of this introduction talks about the main issue—the negative effects of television. The *main issue* sentence is usually at the end of the introduction. When you mention the issue here you should avoid copying too many words from the *question paragraph*. If you copy long phrases or sentences, these will be ignored by the marker and they will not count towards the 250 words you need to write.

Apart from giving the main issue, if you want to write a slightly longer introduction you could add a first sentence which says something very general about the topic. In the example from the Demonstration essay, the first sentence does this.

The conclusion

Like the introduction, the conclusion of your essay should be short, just one or two sentences. The content of the conclusion is more flexible. You can:

- mention the main point of your essay again (in different words)
- give your opinion strongly
- talk about future effects or consequences
- make any other comment that you think is relevant.

Because your essay is relatively short, it is not necessary to summarise the ideas or arguments you have used in your essay. Look at the conclusion from the Demonstration essay:

> *In conclusion, I think that something should be done as soon as possible to protect the community from the negative effects of television. If the situation is left to continue as it is, many new problems for individuals and societies will arise in the future.*

The first sentence gives the writer's opinion about one of the main points in the essay. The last sentence talks about future effects or consequences.

Later, when you are working through the sample essays at the end of this section, pay attention to the kinds of things that are mentioned in the conclusions. Eventually, what is relevant to put into the conclusions of essays in an English style will become clearer to you.

The body of the essay

This is the most important part of your essay because it contains your arguments and evidence or examples.

The first sentence of each paragraph in the body of your essay should give the main point of the paragraph, or otherwise indicate clearly to the reader what topic will be discussed in the paragraph. This kind of sentence is called a *topic sentence*. You have seen in the Reading section of this book that the English style for most paragraphs is to have a topic sentence as the first sentence.

In the Demonstration essay, you will see three good examples of paragraphs that start with clear topic sentences.

Paragraph 2: *Individuals can be negatively affected in three ways.*
Paragraph 3: *There are also various negative effects on families and societies.*
Paragraph 4: *There are two key ways to minimise the negative effects described.*

Almost all the body paragraphs written in the sample answers follow this pattern. Having topic sentences at the beginning of paragraphs is the clearest form of organisation in English. It will help the reader follow your line of thinking.

While you are writing your essay, you should show clearly where new paragraphs begin by starting the first line of each paragraph two or three centimetres from the left-hand side of the page. This is called *indenting*. If you do not indent in handwritten work, it may not be clear to the marker where the paragraph divisions are. As a result, the organisation of your essay will not be clear either.

Linking words

Use appropriate linking words to make your writing more cohesive. Linking words such as *firstly, secondly, also, in addition, however, on the other hand,* will help the reader understand your writing. Make sure you know how to use the most common linking words. There is an exercise on linking words at the end of Reading Section 3.

ACTIVITY 37

Using the plan you have already written for Sample question 5, write the essay. Remember to include:

- an introduction

- paragraphs in the body of the essay that start with topic sentences

- a conclusion.

Don't forget the linking words and don't forget to indent.

Time target: 35 minutes per essay

STEP 5—CHECK FOR MISTAKES

You should allow two minutes at the end of the test time to read through your essay and make corrections. This could make a difference to your final score. Use the checklists in Activity 30 (page 116) to help you.

ACTIVITY 38

The following is a sample essay for Sample question 2. The essay has a broad range of grammatical errors in it. Find the errors and make corrections by crossing out and rewriting.

People generally read newspapers to find out world current affairs, and they read magazines to get entertainment. One would expect therefore to find the type of articles that feature the private lifes of famous peoples in magazines, not newspapers. However nowadays, more and more newspapers including stories like these that they are neither informative nor useful.

According to my opinion I think this type of gossip about peoples private lives should not be in newspapers for several reasons. Firstly, the fact for example, Princess Diana is going out with sportsman is not important news. Secondly, if newspaper want to publish articles about the famous people, they should focussing on their public events and achievements. Such as, if there is an article about Princess Diana, it will be about her charity works, which will increase public awareness of important problems. In addition, journalists should made sure they only write about true facts, not just rumour. One should be able to be reliable on newspapers in factual truth.

Magazines on the one hand, focus on social news and therefore I felt it is acceptable for them to contain some features about famous personalities. In addition to being popular reading, these stories often benefit the stars by being free publicity for them, thereby so helping their career. However I'm also believe that magazine stories should not have mention things that are too embarrassed or untrue, just to attracted people to buy the magazine. Sensational stories like these and causing great unhappy to the person concerned.

In conclusion I think newspapers should concentrate on really news, but magazines can feature some articles on peoples private lives.

Check your corrections with the Answer Key.

ACTIVITY 39

Read the essay you wrote for Sample question 5 (Activity 37) and correct any mistakes you find. Remember: the quickest way to make corrections is to draw a line through the old word(s) and write the new one(s) above.

Time target: 2 minutes per essay

ACTIVITY 40

Using your own plan for Sample question 6 (from Activity 36), write the complete essay. Then check what you have written and make changes as necessary.

Time target: 40 minutes

When you have finished, compare your essay with the sample in the Answer Key.

Summary of the Writing Test

STEP 1—ANALYSE THE QUESTION

TASK 1
- Underline key words
- What is the topic or situation?
- What style should be used?
- What is the purpose of the letter?

TASK 2
- Underline key words
- What is the form of the question?
- How do I answer in a relevant way?

STEP 2—MAKE NOTES OF IDEAS

TASKS 1 and 2

- Take 2 minutes to write down *any* ideas which *may* be relevant
- Be as brief as possible

STEP 3—MAKE A PLAN

TASKS 1 and 2
- Choose relevant ideas
- Support you ideas with relevant examples where possible

STEP 4—WRITE THE ESSAY OF LETTER

TASK 1
- Write an appropriate beginning and ending to your letter
- Write in the correct style
- Use the correct pattern of organisation
- Use the correct functional language
- Use linking words
- Indent paragraphs

TASK 2
- Write an introduction, but do not copy too many words from the question
- Start each paragraph in the body of your essay with a topic sentence
- Use linking words
- Indent paragraphs
- Write a conclusion

STEP 5—CHECK FOR MISTAKES

TASKS 1 and 2
- Allow at least two minutes to correct careless mistakes

Assessing Your Own Writing

Assessing your own writing can be difficult. The following guidelines may help you to measure your progress and isolate your areas of weakness. If you can honestly answer *yes* to most of the following questions, your score should be quite high; if most of the responses are *no*, you have some work to do to avoid a low score.

Content	Organisation	Language
• Have I done what the question asked me to do? • Is it the right length? **Task 1** • Have I included all the necessary information? • Is it written in the correct style? **Task 2** • Does my essay contain some good ideas and opinions which are relevant to the question? • Have I supported my ideas and opinions with examples?	• Is it easy to read ? • Have I presented my ideas and/or information in a logical order? • Is it divided into appropriate paragraphs? • Have I used linking words correctly?	• Have I used a variety of sentence structures? • Are the sentences grammatically accurate? • Is the spelling and punctuation correct? • Is there a range of vocabulary?

Students' Questions Answered

The Writing Test

Can I use a pencil or do I have to use a pen?	It's up to you. You can use whatever you like as long as it is legible.
Do I have to count my words?	No, but it is a good idea to know roughly how many words you usually write to a line. Then you can count the number of lines you write.
What will happen if I don't write enough words?	If you have not answered the questions as completely as you should, you will get a lower score.
What will happen if I write too many words?	If you write far too many words, you might include irrelevant information and/or ideas for which you may be penalised. Also, if you write far too many words for one of the tasks, you may neglect the other.
Is spelling important?	Spelling is important, although the occasional minor mistake won't matter.

Can I start with Task 2 first?	You can do the test in any order. Just make sure you keep to the times advised.
What should I do if I don't understand the question?	You cannot ask the invigilator or use a dictionary. You will have to guess and answer as well as you can.
What's the best way to correct any mistakes that I make?	The quickest way to correct mistakes is to cross them out and write the correction clearly next to or above the mistake.
Will I lose marks if my essay is very messy with lots of crossings out?	No, you won't. But you must make sure that it is legible. Obviously the easier your essay is to read, the happier the examiner will be.
What do I do if I realise I have forgotten to include something important in one of my essays?	You can add it in afterwards, by writing it at the bottom of your essay and showing where it should go with an asterisk or an arrow.
What do I do if I don't know anything about the topic in Task 2?	You will have to do the best you can. Take a few minutes to note down some ideas. Once you start, more details will almost certainly come. (See Step 2 in the Writing section.)
If I don't have enough time to finish, should I finish in note form, like a plan?	No. Anything written in note form will not be read. Just continue in sentences.
Should I memorise answers to a variety of general topics?	No. Anything that the examiner suspects is copied will not count towards the number of words, and you may also be penalised for copying.
Should I write on every other line?	If you have very large writing it might be a good idea. However, for average sized writing it is not necessary because there is still room to make corrections.
I can't write very quickly. What should I do?	You don't actually have to write a lot in the time allowed (400 words in one hour is less than 10 words a minute). However, you should practise writing to time as often as possible, to improve your speed.

GENERAL TRAINING WRITING

PRACTICE TEST 1

TIME ALLOWED: 1 hour

WRITING TASK 1

You should spend no more than 20 minutes on this task.

An Australian colleague is going to your country for a conference. He/She will spend several days in your home town, and has written a letter to you asking for advice about things to see and do there.

Write a letter to the colleague suggesting what he/she should see and do while he/she is in your home town.

You should write at least 150 words.

You do NOT need to write your own address.

WRITING TASK 2

You should spend no more than 40 minutes on this task.

As part of a class assignment you have been asked to write about the following topic.

In Western countries, people spend a lot of money on their pets. They buy special food for their cats or dogs, buy them toys and often pay high fees for medical treatment. Some people think this is a waste of money, and argue that pets are dirty and dangerous.

What are the advantages and disadvantages of having a pet? Do people spend too much money on pets?

Give reasons for your answer.

You should write at least 250 words.

GENERAL TRAINING WRITING

PRACTICE TEST 2

TIME ALLOWED: 1 hour

WRITING TASK 1

You should spend no more than 20 minutes on this task.

Last year you attended an intensive English course at the Darwin College of English. Your new employer has asked you to provide copies of your reports and assignments as quickly as possible.

Write to the director of the language school and request these documents.

You should write at least 150 words.

WRITING TASK 2

You should spend no more than 40 minutes on this task.

As part of a class assignment you have been asked to write about the following topic.

There have been many technological developments in the 20th century, for example in transport, telecommunications and health.

What technological development do you think has been the most important? How has it changed people's lives? Have all the changes been positive?

Give reasons for your answer.

You should write at least 250 words.

GENERAL TRAINING WRITING

PRACTICE TEST 3

TIME ALLOWED: 1 hour

WRITING TASK 1

You should spend no more than 20 minutes on this task.

You booked a two-week holiday to Sydney with Fly-by-Night Travel. You are not happy with the holiday—the flight was delayed, the hotel was noisy, and so on.

Write to Fly-by-Night Travel to complain about the holiday giving details about the problems. Request some compensation or refund.

You should write at least 150 words.

WRITING TASK 2

You should spend no more than 40 minutes on this task.

As part of a class assignment you have been asked to write about the following topic.

In many countries the problem of drug-taking is increasing. Governments and the general public are particularly concerned about young people using illegal drugs such as marijuana, ecstasy and heroin.

What methods could be used to prevent young people from taking drugs? Is it appropriate to send young drug-users to prison?

Give reasons for your answer.

You should write at least 250 words.

GENERAL TRAINING WRITING

PRACTICE TEST 4

TIME ALLOWED: 1 hour

WRITING TASK 1

You should spend no more than 20 minutes on this task.

You have lost your credit card.

Write to the manager of your bank. Explain where and how you lost the card and any other relevant details. Ask the manager to cancel the old card and to send you a replacement.

You should write at least 150 words.

WRITING TASK 2

You should spend no more than 40 minutes on this task.

As part of a class assignment you have been asked to write about the following topic.

Last year many famous pop and sports stars earned millions of dollars each. Many other entertainment and sports personalities also have very high incomes. On the other hand, most people in 'ordinary' professions like nurses, doctors and teachers earn only a small fraction of the incomes of these 'stars'.

What do you think about stars receiving very high salaries? Is it fair that people with jobs that directly help people are paid much less?

Give reasons for your answer.

You should write at least 250 words.

GENERAL TRAINING WRITING

PRACTICE TEST 5

TIME ALLOWED: 1 hour

WRITING TASK 1

You should spend no more than 20 minutes on this task.

A friend is already attending a TAFE college in Australia. You will be going to Australia next year.

Write and ask him/her about what you should do before you go. Ask him/her about any problems he/she has had.

You should write at least 150 words.

WRITING TASK 2

You should spend no more than 40 minutes on this task.

As part of a class assignment you have been asked to write about the following topic.

The average British child between the ages of 4 and 15 watches more than 20 hours of television a week. Studies show she/he only spends about 7 hours per week on physical exercise.

How does this compare with the situation in your country? How can parents make sure children get enough exercise?

Give reasons for your answer.

You should write at least 250 words.

Appendix

Answer Key

The Reading Test

SECTION 1

Activity 1

1. **D** The answer is in the title—*Heart Attack*

2. **4** The subheading *Signs of a heart attack* is followed by four points. Each point describes one symptom.

3. Any two of the following—*smoking, not enough exercise, (high) blood pressure, bad diet, being overweight, (too much) stress*—are correct. The subheading *Preventing a heart attack* is followed by six things you should do to keep your heart healthy. It is logical that not doing them will be bad for your heart.

4. **F** The illustration shows someone in a half-sitting, half-lying position. The words above the picture tell you to 'put the patient in this position'. We can assume that the position shown in the picture is a good one.

Activity 2

1. **C** The answer is written on the sign in the picture, and is mentioned specifically in the third paragraph: 'children's travel-sickness tablets'.

2. 'local chemist' or 'drugstore' The answer is in the italic print near the end of the text.

3. 'children' The word 'junior' is in the drawing, and a number of times the word 'children' is mentioned in the text.

Activity 3

The candidate got the **answers** to all of the questions correct but the **form** of the answers was not always correct. Questions 1, 4 and 8 are answered in the correct way. Questions 2, 3, 5, 6 and 7 are answered in the wrong way.

2. The candidate wrote 5 words. The instruction said NO MORE THAN THREE WORDS.

3. The candidate wrote 6 words. The instruction was NO MORE THAN THREE WORDS.

5. The candidate wrote 'T'. The instructions were to write TRUE.

6. The candidate wrote 'no information'. The instruction was to write NOT GIVEN.

7. The candidate wrote 'one, two or three'. The instructions were to write the letter.

Activity 4

1. green vegetables. The text only gives one source.
2. niacin
3. vitamin B12
4. 10 mcg

Activity 5

1. 6 (times)

Activity 6

1. TRUE
   Key words in the question are *for land, sea, or air travel*. The picture shows a car, a plane and a boat and the text (first sentence) states 'If you travel by bus, car, boat, plane or train … Take a packet of EASY RIDERS.'
2. FALSE
   The key word in the question is *chocolates*. In the third sentence it says 'EASY RIDERS are chocolate-flavoured', which means that they are not chocolates.
3. NOT GIVEN
   Key words in the question are *overdose … not dangerous*. The word 'overdose' is the end of the fourth sentence. The sentence tells us that 'the tablets contain doses (amounts of medicine) that are safe for children'. This means that each tablet contains a small amount of medicine so a child can take the correct dosage without the risk of an overdose.
4. D   In paragraph 5: 'can give EASY RIDERS…as a preventative measure' (something that is done to prevent, or stop something happening), or 'wait … if travel sickness develops … give one'.

Activity 7

1. casualty
2. monitor
3. shed excess pounds
4. shortness of breath
5. sudden onset
6. strain

Activity 8

1. B   The text begins: 'A heart attack is caused by a reduction (decrease) in the blood supply to the heart muscles'.
2. B   Look at the symptoms listed under the subheading *Signs of a heart attack*. The text says that the pain 'could be confused with indigestion', meaning the victim may think, mistakenly, that it is indigestion.
3. medical help / an ambulance
   At the end of paragraph 1, 'call medical help immediately', or under the heading *Action to take*, you find 'call an ambulance'.
4. heartbeat and breathing
   Under the heading *Action to take*, you find: 'Call an ambulance. Check the heartbeat and breathing'. You don't see the word 'casualty' in the text at this point, but it does occur elsewhere, and it should be possible to guess that, in this context, it means the person who has had the heart attack.
5. TRUE
   The logical place to look for information is in the *Action to take* section. At the beginning of the second paragraph, it says 'move gently and as little as possible'.
6. FALSE
   Find 'semi-recumbent' in the text and read 'is the best … takes some of the strain off the heart'—it reduces the strain.
7. NOT GIVEN
   Look under the heading *Action to take*. Paragraph 3 begins with the words 'Loosen any clothing around the neck' but it doesn't say what the effect of this is.

SECTION 2

Activity 9

1. e   is the best answer.
2. g or f
3. i   'with others' implies 'with other students'.

4. **j** timetables organise your hours of study.
5. **a** or **b** The words 'attitude', 'stress' and 'self-confidence' imply personal and psychological factors.

Activity 10
1. paragraphs 2 or 3
    The key words are 'degrees normally last 3 years' and 'first degree courses … take longer'.
2. paragraph 3
    Key words are 'professional training'.
3. paragraph 4
4. paragraph 5
    Key words are 'range of teaching methods'.
5. paragraphs 6 or 7
    Key words are 'assessment of students' work' and 'continuous assessment'.

Activity 11
1. NOT GIVEN
    Paragraphs c, d and (possibly) e discuss revision, but there is no mention of daily review.
2. FALSE
    see paragraphs f and g
3. TRUE
    see paragraph i
4. FALSE
    see paragraph j
5. TRUE
    see paragraph b

Activity 12
1. four years
    see paragraph 2
2. sandwich courses
    see paragraph 3
3. two years
    see paragraph 4
4. seminars
    see paragraph 5
5. continuous assessment
    see paragraph 7

Activity 13
1. **i** Key words are 'limited budget' and 'pay for education and living expenses'.

2. **viii** Key words are 'looking after themselves' and 'without the family's support'.
3. **ii** Key words are 'problems communicating freely' and 'reading and writing in English'.
4. **v** Key words are 'differences in the style and learning between Western and Asian countries'.
5. **iii** Key words are 'racial intolerance' and 'low level of contact'.

Activity 14
1. **g** Key words are 'arranging window displays', 'stock control' and 'retail trade'.
2. **f** Key words are 'Stop Press', 'story', 'news', 'paper' and 'dailies'.
3. **c** Key words are 'a non-profit making service for the sick and elderly'.
4. **h** Key words are 'computers' and 'explain … data bases'.
5. **e** Key words are 'hair cut, styled …' and 'beauty business'.

Activity 15
1. a
2. b
3. h
4. c
5. a

SECTION 3
Activity 16
Note: your answers for this activity may not use exactly the same words as those in the table. The important thing is for the meaning to be the same or similar.

Paragraph	Main topic
1	The nature of the crisis
2 & 3	Statistics on the growing numbers of elderly people
4 & 5	The costs of nursing
6	Medicare
7	Publicly funded programs
8	Private insurance—individual plans

9–11	Private insurance—employer-sponsored plans
12	The ultimate cost to individuals

H	Rules to reduce anxiety and stress

Activity 17
1. 5   *see* paragraph 3
2. 22   *see* paragraph 3
3. $19 000   *see* paragraph 4
    'mean income' means average income
4. 100 000   *see* paragraph 8
    'the number of those over 65 … today is … approximately 100 000'

Activity 18
1. **I**   *see* paragraph 8
    'Individual policies … are currently the most widely available coverage'
2. **M**   *see* paragraph 6
    'mistakenly believe Medicare covers long-term chronic care'
3. **P**   *see* paragraph 7
    'The substantial extra expenditure of a publicly funded program would certainly lose votes.'
4. **E**   *see* paragraph 10
    'Providing for long-term care insurance through employer groups can help lower plan costs'

Activity 19
Note: your answers for this activity may not use exactly the same words as those below. The important thing is for the meaning to be the same or similar.

Paragraph	Main topic
A	Introduction
B	The ways that injuries happen
C	Statistics on deaths and injuries
D	An example from the United States
E and F	Stress-related injuries
G	Rules to prevent physical injuries

Activity 20
1. **B**   'Being struck by a robot arm in motion … the main hazards that robots pose to humans.'
2. **H**   'rules that will help reduce robot-related anxieties'
3. **E**   'workers may suffer from ulcers, colitis and emotional stress'
4. **C**   'Each year, approximately five or six workers are injured'
5–6. **ii** and **iv**   (the order is not important)
    see paragraph E
7. International Labour Office
    see paragraph A
8. leave an area   *see* paragraph G

Activity 21
1. despite
2. workers   *see* paragraphs C and D
3. death
4. stress-related   *see* paragraphs E and F
5. in order to   *see* paragraph H
6. rules   *see* paragraphs G and H

Activity 22
3. **B**   the letters *i.e.* indicate definition or explanation
4. **G**   lack of water is a problem—paragraph C talks about problems and mentions 'water supply'
7. Jakarta   *see* paragraph F
8. 500 million   *see* paragraph C
9. now   *see* paragraph G
12. rural   *see* paragraph H
13. reducing   *see* paragraph H

Activity 23

Sequence	Addition	Example
finally firstly secondly then next after this	as well even in addition also besides this as well as and	for example such as for instance

Reason/Cause	Consequence/Result	Contrast
the cause be the result of because of this since due to this be caused by this because result from	so that so therefore as a result consequently	but however though although while despite even though whereas on the other hand

The Writing Test

TASK 1

Activity 24
Sample question 2

Topic/Situation	you have left a bag in a hotel
Addressee	the manager of the hotel
Purpose	• enquire about the bag—has it been found? • describe the bag • ask the manager to reply • tell the manager how to contact you • explain how the bag should be sent

Sample question 3

Topic/Situation	you had dinner in an expensive restaurant where the food and service were bad
Addressee	the manager of the restaurant
Purpose	• explain the problems you had in the restaurant • give details • ask for some sort of compensation

Activity 26

Plan 3 is the best. Plan 1 focuses on information that is not so important and is not organised into logical groups. Plan 2 does not seem to have any grouping—the order of the points does not seem logical.

Activity 27

- when
    complain
- table (first problem)
    where
    noisy
- service (second problem)
    soup
    dessert
    slow
- food (third problem)
    steak
    vegetables
    sick
    compensation
    hear soon

Activity 28

Plan 1—The task says 'Ask the manager to do something about the situation'. This plan does not include any request for action.

Plan 2—The task says 'Explain these problems'. The problems specifically mentioned in the task are 'terrible service, bad and overpriced food'. This plan does not include details about the *service*.

Activity 30

If one of those dates is convenient, please let me know.

They don't get enough exercise.

A party for all new students will be held on Monday.

Both children and adults are affected.

There are many new problems for individuals.

I am afraid that I have lost your invitation.

There are various negative effects on families and society.

Many of the TV programs in my country come from overseas.

Yesterday, I asked my lecturer about the test results.

Individuals can be negatively affected by television.

Therefore, I must spend the day studying.

Watching too much TV can make people lazy.

Governments should exercise more control.

I hope that your party will be successful.

The cat died, causing great unhappiness.

Thank you for your kind invitation.

My supervisor's party was great.

The ceremony is on the 5th and 6th of February.

I am dreading my first semester economics exam.

I like listening to people's problems.

This is a complicated subject.

He comes from another part of the country.

Activity 31

Dear Mr Simpson,

I stayed in your hotel on the 23rd and the 24th of October. I was in room 603. When I arrived home I discovered that I had left one of my bags at the hotel. Could you please check your Lost and Found department and see if my bag is there?

The bag is a small, black leather, document case with a narrow strap. Inside the bag you will find several business cards, a Mont Blanc fountain pen, a small address book and three copies of a business proposal. Also, a silver pocket calculator. These things are not very valuable in money terms but they have a lot of personal value.

I would appreciate it if you could contact me as soon as possible, particularly since I need the proposals for a presentation this week. If you could send the bag to me by courier service I would be most grateful. I have arranged to pay for the service on delivery.

Thank you for you help.

Yours sincerely,

Fatima Ferrangites

Activity 33

Dear Sir/Madam,

My family and I had dinner in your restaurant on Monday, 28th February. I am writing to you to complain about the food and the service.

The first problem was that, although we had booked a table, we were squashed around a small table at the back of the restaurant near the toilet. It was very noisy and unpleasant.

Secondly, during and after our meal the service was bad. The waiter who delivered soup to my wife had his thumb in it. Another waiter spilt some custard on my mother-in-law's lap. In general, the waiters were rude and the service was slow.

Finally, even though the reputation of your restaurant is good, the food was mediocre. The steak was tough, the vegetables were over-cooked and the desserts were stale. The food was definitely not good value for the price. Also, I think some of the food was bad because I and two members of my family had stomach-aches the following day.

Since we feel we should be compensated somehow, we ask you to refund the cost of our meal. A copy of the bill is enclosed.

I hope to receive your reply shortly.

Yours faithfully,

C. Skate

TASK 2

Activity 34

Sample question 5

You **should** talk about:
- reasons why private information is or is not appropriate in newspapers
- reasons why private information is or is not appropriate in magazines.

Sample question 6

You **should** talk about:
- the short-term and long-term benefits of studying overseas
- the academic and personal benefits of studying overseas
- the problems that students might face while they are studying overseas

Activity 35

Sample question 5	Sample question 6
newspapers • celebrities—not important news • should focus on informing readers • should examine issues *magazines* • entertainment/ popular • benefit the stars • should not feature untrue or embarrassing stories	*academic benefits* • standard • resources • teachers • qualifications *personal benefits* • culture • language • maturity • independence *problems* • study problems • culture shock very different • readjustment • climate, food

Activity 38

Generally, people read newspapers to find out about world current affairs and they read magazines to be entertained. Therefore, one would expect to find articles that feature the private lives of famous people in magazines rather than newspapers. However, nowadays, more and more newspapers include stories like these which are neither informative nor useful.

In my opinion, this type of gossip about people's private lives should not be in newspapers for several reasons. Firstly, for example, the fact that Princess Diana is going out with a sportsman is not important news. Secondly, if newspapers want to publish articles about famous people they should focus on their public events and achievements. In other words, if there is an article about Princess Diana it should be about her works of charity, which will increase public awareness of important problems. In addition, journalists should make sure that they write about the facts only, not rumours. One should be able to rely on newspapers for the actual truth.

Magazines, on the other hand, focus on social news so I feel it is more acceptable for them to contain some features about famous personalities. In addition to being popular reading, these stories often benefit the stars by giving free publicity to them, thereby helping their careers. However, I also believe that magazine stories should not mention things that are too embarrassing or untrue just to attract people to buy the magazine. Sensational stories, such as these, cause great unhappiness to the people concerned.

In conclusion, I think newspapers should concentrate on real news but magazines can feature some articles on people's private lives.

Activity 40

Studying overseas has clear advantages, but it is not without its problems.

The main benefits of studying overseas are academic ones. Generally, the standard of education is higher. This is because colleges and universities have up-to-date equipment and other resources. Also, teachers and lecturers are highly-skilled professionals who are aware of all the latest developments in their fields of interest. A final point is that the qualifications which a student obtains are valid usually anywhere in the world.

As well as the obvious academic benefits, students also gain experience of another culture, improve their language skills and meet many new people. Thus, they will develop many interpersonal skills and become more tolerant. They will become more emotionally mature as they deal with living apart from their family. This helps their personal development as they become more independent.

Although, in some cases, there are some negative effects. Most importantly, if students are not properly prepared academically before they go abroad, they could have difficulties following lectures or writing assignments. Furthermore, young students may have problems adjusting to a new culture and could experience loneliness and homesickness. A final problem could be that they adapt so much to Western culture that they have problems readjusting when they finally return home.

Other possible problems are difficulties in adjusting to a different climate, different food and different lifestyle. With appropriate preparation and support most students should be able to avoid or overcome these obstacles.

However, in general, I consider the advantages of an overseas education much greater than any of the disadvantages described above.

Reading Practice Tests

PRACTICE TEST 1

1. **C**   Key words are 'pay' and 'cash'.
2. **E**   Key word is 'how' and E explains a system.
3. **D**   Key word is 'advance'.
4. **F**   Key words are 'number of tickets, ideal for groups'.
5. **B**   Key words are 'rock concerts'.
6. TRUE   'potentially fatal'
7. NOT GIVEN   'The text mentions that children should have injections.
8. FALSE   'have regular tetanus injections, a booster … every five years'.
9. TRUE   'They are more prone to falling over and getting dirt in wounds than adults.'
10. **D**   'pick up a copy'.
11. **C**   'most important feature of the new card system is card reusability'.
12. **A**   'return the card along with a cash payment for the amount of credit you want added'.
13. **i**   'study materials, etc'.
14. **iii**   'tasks to do outside of class time'.
15. **v**   'passing your course … '
16. **x**   'attend 65% or more etc'.
17. **viii** 'will receive a letter of attendance/will receive a certificate of achievement'.
18. **vii**   'become a member of the college library'.
19. residential colleges
    There is no kitchen.
20. gas and electricity
    Section B, second sentence.

21. size, condition, location
Section D, third sentence (*not* paragraph 2 which talks about all types of accommodation).
22. a residential college
Section C: 'a feature of many academic institutions, located on campus'.
23. damage property
Paragraph after section D, second sentence.
24. receipt   Rule 4
25. understand it   Rule 1
26. **K**   *see* first sentence
27. **F**   *see* first sentence
28. **E**   *see* first sentence
29. **C**   *see* last sentence
30. **G**   *see* last 3 sentences
31. Mugunga Camp   *see* paragraph D
32. Gitarama   *see* paragraph G
33. UNICEF   *see* paragraph M
34. Myra Adamson   *see* paragraph J
35. running an orphanage   *see* paragraph K
36. FALSE   *see* paragraph I and the last sentence of paragraph J
37. NOT GIVEN
38. TRUE   *see* paragraph C, last sentence: 'FHI supported groups of unaccompanied children.'
39. FALSE   *see* paragraph K—only about 40% are in orphanages
40. TRUE   *see* paragraph D. Key words are 'originally', 'children separated from their families, Rwandan refugees'.

PRACTICE TEST 2

1. **C**   'As a civil engineering charity ...'
2. **B**   'Over 20 million ... in Britain ... is projected to at least double by the year 2025.'
3. several hundred miles   *see* paragraph 5
4. (the) road dangers
'astonished at the road dangers we put up with here.'
5. slower traffic systems   *see* paragraph 8
6. by donating money/make a decision
see last 2 sentences
7. walkers   *see* paragraph 5
8. TRUE   'traffic through country areas might treble by then' (2025)
9. TRUE   'WHO limits are regularly exceeded in most UK cities.'

10. FALSE   'Four times as many junior-age children are driven to school in Britain as in Germany.'
11. TRUE   '1 in 7 children suffers from asthma, thought to be exacerbated (made worse) by traffic fumes.'
12. NOT GIVEN
The network will go through cities but that does not mean that most of the network will be rural.
13. FALSE   'The National Network will ... run right through the middle of most major towns and cities.'
14. FALSE   'Cost the equivalent (same) as just a few weeks of the current national roads program.'
15. i   Key words are 'deciding which program'.
16. iv   Key words are 'tuition fees'.
17. viii   Key words are 'full details of term dates'.
18. ix   Key words are 'overseas student office'.
19. vii   Key words are 'help graduates find suitable employment'.
20. iii   Key words are 'the few regulations that are enforced are ...'
21. immigration authorities (point two)
22. an ELICOS course (point three)
23. the students (*see* Fees, point 2: 'textbooks, equipment ... are your responsibility')
24. by bankdraft   (*see* Fees, point 4)
25. it is refunded   (*see* Application fees, point b)
26. over 4 weeks   (*see* Course fees, point c)
27. International Student Programs
(*see* Transfer to Another Institution)
28. **B**   'the surviving panda population has also become fragmented, panda "islands"... separated'.
29. **D**   'the bamboo that is their staple food'.
30. **E**   'better control of poaching, which remains a problem despite strict laws'.
31. **A**   'Deforestation, mainly carried out by farmers clearing land to make way for fields ... has drastically contracted the mammal's range'.

32. **ii**   *see* paragraph C
33. **vi**   *see* paragraph B
34. decreased   *see* paragraph A
35. disconnected   *see* paragraph B
36. problems   *see* paragraph C
37. growth   *see* paragraph D
38. join   *see* paragraph E
39. reserves   *see* paragraph E
40. cooperate   *see* paragraph F

PRACTICE TEST 3

1. **B**   Key words are 'save money and earn interest, money box, passbook'.
2. **C**   'every six months.'
3. FALSE   'some medical type operations performed by approved dentists are covered.'
4. NOT GIVEN
5. TRUE   'if you need to see a specialist you must be referred by your doctor.'
6. TRUE   *see* Public Patients *and* Private Patients *sections.*
7. by surface mail   *see* the paragraph headed *Getting the Price Right*, second sentence.
8. 35 p   *see* the paragraph headed *Stamp Books*, third sentence.
9. barcode technology   *see* the introductory sentence in the *Priority Treatment* section: 'to track and trace your mail'.
10. international registered   section 2 'valuables' means *expensive items*.
11. sign on delivery   *see* the first sentence of sections 1 and 2.
12. courier service   *see* last sentence of *Swiftair*, section 3.
13. **I**   'diverse uses that candles and other wax products can be put to' (*not* D which has only wax models).
14. **C**   'native birds and other wildlife' (*not* B which features 'exotic' animals).
15. **F**   'features of the night sky; origin of the crab nebula'.
16. **D**   'anyone interested in changing trends in clothing'.

17. **A**   'hands-on information technology'.
18. **E**   'recorded on tape ... interested in art history and criticism'.
19. **J**   'entered via the River Widmore'.
20. TRUE   'TAFE is the largest of the tertiary education sectors' (*see* paragraph 2).
21. TRUE   'the qualifications they award are transferable throughout Australia' (*see* paragraph 3).
22. FALSE   'TAFE colleges cannot award tertiary-level (university) degrees' (*see* paragraph 3).
23. FALSE   'These private institutions are like TAFE colleges ... but each one of them usually specialises in courses for one industry' (*see* paragraph 5).
24. TRUE   Vocational Training is Chapter 5, English language is Chapter 6 (*see* paragraph 6).
25. FALSE   *see* paragraph 7, first and second sentences.
26. BOTH   *see* paragraph 5, third sentence and paragraph 10, third sentence.
27. **UGG**   *see* paragraph 10
28. **AC**   *see* paragraph 7
29. **AC**   *see* paragraph 5, third sentence.
30. NEITHER   *see* paragraph 12, last sentence; paragraph 13, first sentence.
31. of land shortages   *see* paragraph 1, first sentence; paragraph 2.
32. trees and parks   *see* paragraph 5, last sentence.
33. office space   *see* paragraph 7.
34. not available yet   *see* paragraph 12.
35. grid station   *see* paragraph 10.
36. downtown   *see* paragraph 8.
37. leisure   *see* paragraph 6, which talks about parks, entertainment, fitness areas and shopping.
38. network   *see* paragraph 10 (network = grid).
39. obstacle   *see* paragraph 11.
40. ground   *see* paragraph 11.

Note: the following essays are examples only. Your own essay may
- use different language
- provide different details, explanations and/or examples
- be organised differently (Task 2 essays only)
- have a different opinion (Task 2).

PRACTICE TEST 1

TASK 1

This letter *gives information.*

Introductory paragraph—thank the addressee if he or she has sent you a letter

Give information

More information

Closing paragraph—say you hope you have been helpful. Offer to provide more information

> Dear Dr. Milson,
>
> Thank you for your letter. I was very pleased to hear you will be visiting Jakarta and hope the following information will help you to enjoy your stay.
>
> First of all, Jakarta is a big and busy city, the centre of government and business. There are many international quality hotels and restaurants as well as shopping centres, markets and entertainment places.
>
> However, I think you would like to see some places that are unique to my country. I know you are interested in art and history so firstly I suggest you visit Monas, which is the Independence monument. Secondly, not far from Monas you can find the National Museum which has a large collection of art, textiles and other cultural items.
>
> Other interesting places are a 'wayang' museum, which features our unique shadow-puppet dramas, and Pasar Ikan (the fish market) where you can see traditional fishing boats.
>
> I hope these suggestions have been helpful. As you only have a short time in Jakarta, you probably will not be able to do much more sightseeing. But if I can help in any other way, please let me know.
>
> Yours sincerely,
>
> Ari

TASK 2

To answer this question in a relevant way you have to:
- describe the advantages and disadvantages of having a pet
- say whether or not people spend too much money on pets.

Short introduction

Advantages

> In many Western homes people keep a dog or cat or some other kind of pet. While this does involve some expense in terms of good food and medical treatment, there are still many advantages to keeping a pet.
>
> First of all, pets are good companions. This is especially important for people who live alone and for older people who do not go out much. Some pets can also help to protect the house from thieves. Secondly, dogs and cats like to play and can give hours of amusement to children and adults. Taking care of an animal also helps children to develop responsible attitudes and to learn about nature. Finally, the actual expense of keeping an animal is not that high, and they can eat the left-overs of family meals.

Disadvantages—including counter arguments against those disadvantages	Some people claim pets are dirty. I don't think this is altogether true. Responsible pet owners keep their pets clean and healthy so they do not smell bad. People also say that certain pets, like large dogs, can be dangerous. There have been cases of dogs attacking and seriously injuring small children. However, these cases are uncommon and are the result of bad owners. These people either don't train their dogs properly or actually encourage them to be aggressive. So, the problems of pets being unclean or dangerous are in fact the problems of the owners, not the pets themselves.
Short conclusion	To sum up, there are more advantages than disadvantages to keeping a pet, especially for lonely people and children. In most cases, therefore, the cost is justified.

PRACTICE TEST 2

TASK 1

This letter *makes a request.*

Introductory paragraph— explain your reason for writing. Tell the addressee who you are	Dear Ms. Abbott, I am writing to ask for your assistance. I attended a 3-week English course at your college from 6 November to 24 November, 1995. My full name is Syarif Mustafa and my student number was CZ 352Z. The course I attended was English for Travel and Tourism at intermediate level. My class instructors were Robin Tyson and Alice Maddax.
Explain the situation	I am about to start work at Suntours travel company and they have asked me to provide information about the English course and any assignments and reports. Unfortunately, I left all my copies of these documents at my friend's house and cannot contact him at present.
Give details of your request	Therefore, I would be very grateful if you could send me copies of the course outline, the three written assignments and the end of course report as soon as possible. I will be happy to refund any postal charges.
Closing paragraph—mention what the addressee will do	Thank you so much for your help in this matter. I look forward to receiving the copy course outlines. Yours sincerely, Waldo Emerson

TASK 2

To answer this question in a relevant way you have to:

- name the *one* technical development you think has been the most important and give reasons why
- describe *how* this development has changed people's lives
- say whether *all* the changes as a result of this development have been positive.

Introductory paragraph— the most important development in technology	In my opinion, television is the most important technological development. Nowadays almost everyone in the world has access to TV. Television has caused significant changes in family life and education. Some of these changes have been positive while others have been negative.
How TV has changed lives in positive ways	Certainly TV can be a powerful educational tool. People can learn about situations and problems far away, and begin to understand different cultures. Many informative documentaries about nature, news, and social issues are made now, and these can stimulate people to action. People in isolated areas can know for them-

How TV has changed lives in negative ways

selves what is happening in the world. This gives them the power to make their own decisions and form their own opinions.

However, the changes have not all been positive. Before television was widely available, families spent more time together talking and playing games. They seemed much closer to each other than modern families. Now, many children even have their own TV in the bedroom so they spend very little time with their parents or brothers and sisters. Some people might argue that this helps young people to become independent, but I think this is a negative effect because they will be unable to communicate effectively or relate to others emotionally.

Also, the fact is that people waste a lot of time watching poor quality programs which do not have a positive influence. People get a bad impression of the real world from such programs. Advertising, too, can have very negative effects. Furthermore, TV is sometimes used to deliberately misinform people, for example when it is used as a propaganda tool by governments.

Short conclusion

To sum up, I feel that, overall, there are strong positive effects of TV in terms of its educational role, but it has in many ways altered people and families in a negative sense.

PRACTICE TEST 3

TASK 1

This letter *makes a complaint.*

Introductory paragraph— explain your reason for writing. Tell the addressee who you are and what their connection is with you

Explain the problems

Dear Mr. Jenkins,

I am writing to complain about my recent holiday in Sydney which was organised by your company. My wife and I selected the two week Women's Weekly tour starting on 29 December. Your agency claimed we would be picked up at the airport, and that the hotel was three-star quality. The all-inclusive price we paid included breakfast and dinner and two excursions.

On arrival at the airport, there was no one to meet us. We waited for half an hour and then had no choice except to take a taxi. This cost $30. The receipt is enclosed.

The hotel was not what I would consider three-star. The room was dirty, the beds were small and uncomfortable. The breakfast portions were very small, and the hotel refused to provide us with dinner. We had to spend a further $500 on extra meals. Again, I enclose our restaurant receipts.

Mention what the addressee will do

I find it dishonest and unacceptable that your company sold us a tour which in no way resembled the description, and my wife and I expect to be compensated for all our extra expenses. The receipts which are enclosed total $530. In addition, we claim a refund of $100 because the room was not up to the promised standard.

We expect to receive your cheque for $630 very soon.

Yours sincerely,

Mr. I. Rate

TASK 2

To answer this question in a relevant way you have to:

- suggest how young people could be discouraged from taking drugs
- say whether it is a good idea to send drug users to prison and give reasons.

<table>
<tr><td>Short introduction</td><td>There have been several anti-drug campaigns in Europe, but they have had generally little or no success. I feel that it is very difficult to stop teenagers experimenting with illegal drugs.</td></tr>
<tr><td>Method—reasons why it failed</td><td>Methods to educate young people about drugs are usually ineffective for a couple of reasons. First of all, these films or talks are designed and presented by authority figures such as teachers or the police. Generally, teenagers react against these people and reject their values. Secondly, the information is often inaccurate and the teenagers actually think they know more about drugs than the 'experts'.</td></tr>
<tr><td>Method and its purpose

Why it failed

Alternative suggestion</td><td>In addition, anti-drug campaigns are often designed by the wrong people. In Britain recently, one anti-drug campaign featured photographs and posters of drug-users. These photographs were supposed to show how unattractive (thin and pale) drug addicts become. In fact, many teenage girls admired the boy featured and used the poster as a pin-up. They thought he was exciting and glamorous. It would be better if anti-drug campaigns were designed by ex-addicts or teenagers with drug problems.</td></tr>
<tr><td>Method and its purpose

Why it failed

Other disadvantages of this method</td><td>Another thing which is supposed to deter young drug-users is the threat of long prison sentences. In my opinion, this is a waste of money and ineffective. Fear of arrest and imprisonment will not deter young people. Young people like to take risks. Also, if they are sent to prison they will meet serious criminals and learn more about crime. They will also develop an anti-social attitude. It is very expensive to put someone in prison and should only be used as a punishment for people who are a danger to society. Drug-users only harm themselves, not other people.</td></tr>
<tr><td>Short conclusion</td><td>So, I can only conclude that no current methods from campaigns to jail sentences are effective. As the drug problem seems to be increasing everywhere, I think governments need to work harder to find a realistic solution.</td></tr>
</table>

PRACTICE TEST 4

TASK 1

This letter *makes a request.*

<table>
<tr><td>Explain your reason for writing. Tell the addressee who you are</td><td>Dear Sir,
    I am writing to confirm the loss of my credit card. I telephoned your office earlier today.</td></tr>
<tr><td>Explain other relevant details</td><td>   The details of my card are as follows. It is an Apex Silver card in the name Jorge Luis Banderas. The credit card number is 4531 7602 2597 8413. I have had an Apex card since 1994. This card is valid from August 1995 to August 1996.</td></tr>
<tr><td>Explain when and how you lost the card</td><td>   I lost the card yesterday at about 10:30 in the evening. The only time I used the card yesterday was to buy three bottles of wine at the Sharp Price Liquor Store in Oxford Street. By accident, I left the card at the shop. When I realised I had done this, I telephoned the shop, but the shop assistants there could not find the card.</td></tr>
<tr><td>Closing paragraph—mention what the addressee will do</td><td>   Could you please cancel my card immediately and make the necessary arrangements to issue me with a replacement card? I can be contacted at the above address.
    Thank you for your assistance.

Yours faithfully,

Jorge Banderas</td></tr>
</table>

TASK 2

To answer this question in a relevant way you have to:
- explain your opinion about stars earning a lot of money
- give an opinion about people like nurses and teachers who have more useful jobs but who earn much less money, and explain your opinion.

Introductory paragraph—state your opinion	It seems that salaries often do not relate to skill, education or the value of the employee to society. In my opinion this is wrong, and I feel changes should be made to ensure that people such as pop stars do not earn such huge amounts of money.
Reasons for the opinion	If we take the example of a pop star such as Madonna, it is hard to see in what way she benefits society. In fact, her behaviour could even have a negative effect on young people and encourage them to experiment with sex and drugs, and develop a materialistic attitude. In addition, her job does not require special skills or years of training and education. Therefore, there is no justification for her receiving so much money. Although she provides entertainment for people, I do not think this can be considered essential.
Answer the second part of the question. Give reasons	On the other hand, there are many professions which not only require high skills and years of education but also help other people and the community in general. Clearly doctors, nurses and teachers are much more useful, in fact, essential to society than entertainment and sports figures. Their salaries should reflect their dedication, and the heavy responsibilities they face in their jobs.
Conclusion—offering a solution	However, even if we accept this idea, the problem of how we could make salaries fairer remains. Pop stars receive royalties from sales of their records or concert tickets. How could this money be taken away and given to more deserving people? Perhaps the only solution is through much higher taxes for people who earn excessively high salaries.

PRACTICE TEST 5

TASK 1

This letter *makes a request*. The style is *informal* because the letter is to a friend.

Greet the addressee	Dear Denny,
Explain the situation	How are you getting on in Melbourne? I hope everything is going well and you are enjoying your studies. I'm writing to ask you for some information as I'm planning to come and study in Australia next year. I have applied to the TAFE college in Adelaide to take the course in Tourism and Hospitality Management.
Give details of your request	Could you tell me what I have to do to obtain a study visa and how long the process will take? The college said I also have to take out insurance before I come to Australia. How do I do this? I'd be really grateful if you can give me this information. I would also be grateful if you can tell me what I should bring with me, for example, clothes, books or anything I cannot get in Australia.
Mention what the addressee will do	I'm sure that studying in a college overseas has not been without at least some problems for you. Adjusting to a new culture was probably also difficult. Have you had any particular problems that I should watch out for? I'd appreciate any advice you can give me.

Many thanks,

Sita |

TASK 2

To answer this question in a relevant way you have to:
- say how long each week children in your country do exercise and watch TV
- say how parents can ensure that their children get enough exercise.

Introductory paragraph	The figures given for the number of hours British children watch TV and exercise are rather disturbing. Clearly children are spending too many hours passively watching TV. Their lack of exercise could lead to health problems such as obesity and may cause severe problems such as heart disease later in life.
Answer to the first part of the question	In my country children generally have a lot more exercise. Most children walk or cycle to and from school. Many children help their parents with housework or farmwork after school and at weekends. Children also spend a lot of time playing sports such as football and volleyball. Besides that, there are not many TV programs which appeal to young people. I imagine most children only watch 1 or 2 hours of TV per week.
Answer to the second part of the question	I think the main solution to children's lack of exercise has to come from their parents. If parents set a good example and take exercise themselves at weekends and exercise with their children, it would seem a natural part of life. In addition, parents could get a dog for their child and insist the child takes the dog for a walk every day. Parents could also buy their child a bicycle or pay for them to join a sports club. Finally, parents could also restrict the number of hours that their children watch TV. Schools can also help to ensure that children get enough exercise. They could timetable sports classes more often. They should also teach children about the importance of having exercise.
Short conclusion	In conclusion, children should be told about the importance of physical exercise, and both parents and schools should motivate them to be active from an early age.

Acknowledgments

The authors wish to thank all those who assisted in creating, commenting on, tampering with, trialling and otherwise contributing to the materials in this book. Our most sincere thanks to Adrian Kelly, Nicky Cousins, Merle Green, Caroline Bentley, Wendy Sahanaya, Liz Hunt, Molly Abott and Kevin Dalton, and the rest of our colleagues who had to put up with us while this project was in progress.

IELTS Reading Answer Sheet

Module taken:

Academic ☐   General Training ☐

Version number:
Please enter the number
in the boxes and shade
the number in the grid

00 10 20 30 40 50 60 70 80 90
☐ ☐ ☐ ☐ ☐ ☐ ☐ ☐ ☐ ☐

0 1 2 3 4 5 6 7 8 9
☐ ☐ ☐ ☐ ☐ ☐ ☐ ☐ ☐ ☐

#		✓ ✗		#		✓ ✗
1		☐₁☐		31		☐₃₁☐
2		☐₂☐		32		☐₃₂☐
3		☐₃☐		33		☐₃₃☐
4		☐₄☐		34		☐₃₄☐
5		☐₅☐		35		☐₃₅☐
6		☐₆☐		36		☐₃₆☐
7		☐₇☐		37		☐₃₇☐
8		☐₈☐		38		☐₃₈☐
9		☐₉☐		39		☐₃₉☐
10		☐₁₀☐		40		☐₄₀☐
11		☐₁₁☐		41		☐₄₁☐
12		☐₁₂☐		42		☐₄₂☐
13		☐₁₃☐		Band Score		Reading Total
14		☐₁₄☐
15		☐₁₅☐
16		☐₁₆☐
17		☐₁₇☐
18		☐₁₈☐
19		☐₁₉☐
20		☐₂₀☐
21		☐₂₁☐
22		☐₂₂☐
23		☐₂₃☐
24		☐₂₄☐
25		☐₂₅☐
26		☐₂₆☐
27		☐₂₇☐
28		☐₂₈☐
29		☐₂₉☐
30		☐₃₀☐

Recommended Self-Study Materials

READING

Baudoin, E. M. *et al*, *Reader's Choice*, 2nd edn, University of Michigan Press, 1986.
Davies E. *et al*. *Task Reading*, Cambridge University Press, 1990.
Haarman, L., Leech, P. & Murray, J., *Reading Skills for the Social Sciences*, Oxford University Press, 1989.
Henke, S., *Skilful Reading*, Prentice Hall, 1981.
Maley, A., *Oxford Supplementary Skills: Reading Intermediate*, Oxford University Press, 1988.
Maley, A., *Oxford Supplementary Skills: Reading Upper Intermediate*, Oxford University Press, 1987.
Mikulecky, B. S. & Jeffries, L., *Reading Power*, Addison Wesley, 1986.
Smith, M. & G. A., *Study Skills Handbook*, 2nd edn, Oxford University Press.
Waters, A. & M., *Study Tasks in English*, Cambridge University Press, 1995.

WRITING

Glendenning, E., *Write Ideas*, Longman, 1983.
Jolly, D., *Writing Tasks*, Cambridge University Press, 1984.
Maley, A., *Oxford Supplementary Skills: Writing Upper Intermediate*, Oxford University Press, 1987.
Oshima, H. & Hogue, A., *Introduction to Academic Writing*, Addison Wesley, 1988.
Rooks, G. M., *Paragraph Power*, Prentice Hall, 1988.
Withrow, J., *Effective Writing*, Cambridge University Press, 1987.

GRAMMAR

Azar, B. S., *Basic English Grammar*, Prentice Hall, 1984.
Eastwood, J., *Oxford Guide to English Grammar*, Oxford University Press, 1994.
Eastwood, J., *Oxford Practice Grammar*, Oxford University Press, 1992.
Eastwood, J. & Mackin, R. A., *Basic English Grammar with Exercises*, Oxford University Press.
Murphy, R., *English Grammar in Use*, Cambridge University Press, 1985.
Murphy, R., *Essential Grammar in Use*, Cambridge University Press.
Swan, M., *Basic English Usage*, Oxford University Press.
Swan, M. & Walter, C., *How English Works*, Oxford University Press, 1997.

VOCABULARY

Cunnningsworth, A. & Fest, P., *Word Power*, Macmillan, 1992.
Macarthy & O'Dell, *English Vocabulary in Use*, Cambridge University Press, 1994.
Redman & Ellis, *A Way with Words* (Books 1, 2 & 3), Cambridge University Press, 1987.
Wellman, G., *Wordbuilder*, Heinemann, 1989.